Sustaining Lean in Healthcare

Developing and Engaging Physician Leadership

Sustaining Lean in Healthcare

Mike Nelson

Endorsements:

"Nelson does lean healthcare a service as a physician and lean practitioner focusing on engaging the physician. In this valuable resource, Nelson stresses and supplies guidance regarding the role of physician champion and senior management's responsibilities to the lean initiative. As importantly, he provides realistic estimates of timelines for projects, expected satisfaction, quality, and financial paybacks, as well as for the time commitments required for lean healthcare initiatives to become durable successes."

David Mann, PhD
Principal, David Mann Lean Consulting

"Nelson's great service in this book is to approach lean healthcare from the practitioner's perspective and provide a very valuable and thoughtful approach which simplifies and organizes the steps needed to effectively and successfully take advantage of the significant contributions lean management can make to their practices with the minimum expenditure of time and financial resources."

Edward D. Martin, MD
Co-Founder and Chairman Emeritus
Martin Blanck & Associates, Inc.

"Over the years, I have read a number of books on lean implementation. Dr Nelson's approach is clear, practical, easy to read and prescriptive. Efficient use of resources and time are some of the most important directives for leaders to survive in these reforming times. Lean has become a critical predictor of successful systems going forward. *Sustaining Lean in Healthcare* is the book to get this done. Well done, Dr. Nelson. I learned a ton."

Stephen C Beeson, MD
Author, Practicing Excellence: A Physician's Manual to Exceptional Health
Care *and* Engaging Physicians: A Manual to Physician Partnership

"Of the many books written about Lean journeys, Mike Nelson's book offers a unique perspective. A physician himself, Mike focuses on the role he and his colleagues can play in creating and sustaining a Lean environment. He speaks from first-hand experience, having taken his own Lean journey and playing a key role in the quality aspect of a highly successful ValuMetrix® Services Lean engagement. His book clearly illustrates a fact that is all-too-often often overlooked – physicians *must* be included in any Lean engagement, since they are true enablers of change and are critical to sustaining the transformation. Instead of writing another how-to book, Mike has taken the opportunity to provide insights that are sure to help any healthcare organization sustain the impact of its Lean engagement."

Rick Malik
Worldwide Director
ValuMetrix® Services

Over the past two decades Lean Operations has made several significant runs in healthcare. The first attempts, with a few notable exceptions, lost momentum and were not sustainable because the incentives always seemed to be misaligned. In this book, Dr. Nelson draws on his forty years of medical practice and his experience as an early adopter of Lean for healthcare to identify a crucial piece to aligning healthcare organizations for success: Physician Engagement. It's my experience that Lean methods work on processes in all industries, but nowhere is the human element more critical to their success than healthcare, and no one role is more critical than the Physician. Healthcare executives and clinicians will appreciate and learn from Dr. Nelson's insight.

Robert Iversen
Director, Accenture Management Consulting

Sustaining Lean in Healthcare

Developing and Engaging Physician Leadership

Michael Nelson, M.D.

Foreword by Quint Studer,
Founder & CEO, Studer Group

CRC Press
Taylor & Francis Group
Boca Raton   London   New York

CRC Press is an imprint of the
Taylor & Francis Group, an **informa** business

A PRODUCTIVITY PRESS BOOK

CRC Press
Taylor & Francis Group
6000 Broken Sound Parkway NW, Suite 300
Boca Raton, FL 33487-2742

© 2011 by Taylor & Francis Group, LLC
CRC Press is an imprint of Taylor & Francis Group, an Informa business

No claim to original U.S. Government works

Printed in the United States of America on acid-free paper

International Standard Book Number: 978-1-4398-4027-6 (Paperback)

Visit the Taylor & Francis Web site at
http://www.taylorandfrancis.com

and the CRC Press Web site at
http://www.crcpress.com

To Patsy, my wonderful wife of 43 years. Not only did she read, edit, and comment on the book, but took numerous chores and duties off my hands in order to give me time to write.

Contents

Acknowledgments

I want to recognize Mike Hogan, a Lean *sensei,* for his technical review and feedback of the book. Joe Calvaruso wrote the chapter on the senior leader roles, and I want to thank him for his contribution. Sherry Gentry and Cheryl Mitchell were kind enough to read the book as it was being written and provide feedback on content as well as grammar. I also want to recognize Cheryl Finske who edited major portions of the book prior to submission to Productivity Press.

Introduction

I started a solo pediatric practice in 1976 in Albuquerque, New Mexico. The loan from the bank to start the practice was basically done with a handshake. The practice was established in a growing but somewhat remote suburb that was at least a 30-minute drive to the nearest hospital, laboratory, or x-ray facility. When I needed a simple x-ray, I would take the children next door to the vet, who had a machine. In return, when he had dying kittens or pups from a C-section, I would help resuscitate them using a modified bulb syringe as an ambu bag. No one expressed any concerns about the practice and some even thought it amusing.

Over time, the practice grew to include seven pediatricians. As the practice grew so did HMOs, formularies, prior authorizations, medication choices, and treatment choices, all of which added to the complexity of providing care to my patients. The number of steps required just to provide simple care seemed to increase exponentially. I found myself spending more and more time at the office in order to complete the same care that used to take far less time.

By the early 1990s my frustration over how hard it was to provide care led me to explore the world of quality improvement to find solutions. I learned and adopted the tools and principles of Total Quality Management (TQM), engineering redesign, Continuous Quality Improvement (CQI), Rapid Improvement Workshops, and even became certified as a Quality Engineer and, eventually, a Lean Six Sigma Black Belt. There were some early improvement successes. Application of a community-acquired pneumonia bundle reached a highly reliable state, only to deteriorate 1–2 years later. An innovative new process using volunteers who reached out to eligible women to increase mammography screening rates worked very well. Again, after a year or so the process was abandoned. Invariably the improvements were not sustained. Over time people reverted to the same old inefficient, non-value-added work that absorbs our personal energy and leaves less and less for us to focus on the patients' needs, let alone keep new improvements sustained into the future. The waste continued to accumulate.

In retrospect, what was happening reminds me of the parable of "The Boiled Frog." The story simply states that if you take a frog and put it in a pot of boiling water, it will immediately jump out. If you put the frog in cold water and very gradually turn up the heat the frog will stay until it boils to death.

As I began to learn about Lean Systems Thinking (Toyota Production Systems[1]), I began to think I might be contributing to time spent on wasteful activities. The time spent looking for materials, supplies, reports, time spent waiting on results of testing performed by others, distances traveled to retrieve necessary equipment, forms, and tools, and recurrent attempts to communicate with patients and peers are all examples of largely hidden waste. We've become desensitized to this type of waste and often no longer "see" the waste. Perhaps after multiple unsuccessful attempts to fix this type of waste in the past it has been relegated to our subconscious minds. We give up and just adapt. So it was that each new step required by the government and insurance companies or quick fixes someone created to work around bad processes was seemingly inconsequential or, at worst, something to complain about over coffee in the physician's lounge; however, the cumulative effect has been dramatic.

In the outpatient setting there is one simple example of this type of waste, regarding the purchase and allocation of everyday tools like thermometers and blood pressure cuffs. The decision to buy a piece of equipment is too often based solely on cost. In my own practice, as overhead costs went up and the practice grew, we determined that perhaps we didn't need all the equipment in each exam room. We could put the equipment in a central place, people could share, and we wouldn't have to buy another piece of expensive equipment. It may have been inconvenient, but, after all, it was usually just a few seconds of my time or the nurse's time to retrieve the necessary tools. In retrospect, I probably interrupted patient visits and left the exam room thousands of time.

Recently, in a four-physician internal medicine practice we measured the amount of time lost from these seemingly inconsequential forays to find needed items. For that practice, the time totaled 2 hours a day of lost productivity for the group. Each physician essentially lost 30 minutes a day, every day of their practice life—time which could have been spent attending to patients' needs. Taken collectively, all of the seemingly inconsequential extra steps lead us to a state where we can easily lose focus on our primary purpose of providing great care.

The road sign in Figure I.1 has become my favorite metaphor for explaining waste in healthcare. We are so distracted and consumed by waste (in this case, the sharp edges of the sign) that it makes it difficult to focus on our primary mission of improving the health of individuals and the population (in the case of the sign, the "Bridge Is Out" message at the bottom of the sign). This waste is in addition to the required regulatory waste, duplicate testing, unnecessary procedures, defensive medicine, etc., that people usually refer to as waste in healthcare. I have come to believe that one of the biggest sources of waste comes from how we go about performing our daily work. I was frustrated and determined to do something about the inefficiencies.

Figure I.1   Roadside sign.

Three years ago I discovered Toyota Production Systems (TPS) or Lean Systems Thinking and assumed a role as learner, implementer, and teacher at Presbyterian Healthcare Services in Albuquerque, New Mexico. Working directly in the outpatient setting and learning from peers working in the ED, inpatient units, and ORs utilizing Lean principles allowed me to really begin to see the enormous waste in healthcare.

I was also able to see the effectiveness of Lean at driving out that waste. The four internists mentioned above voluntarily added 54 appointment slots a week to their schedule after we were able to address their needs for equipment and added value and efficiency through other Lean improvements. The results now have been sustained for 2 years. The story of this clinic is presented in Chapter 9. My personal experiences and knowing the results of others like Virginia Mason and Thedacare were sentinel in my becoming a Lean enthusiast. I am unabashedly "drinking the Lean Kool-Aid."

Lean is totally focused on adding value for our patients. There are strict criteria for determining value (See Chapter 1); however, many of the improvements put in place during a Lean implementation also benefit virtually the entire healthcare workforce. Employees are able to enjoy greater work efficiencies as well as the pleasure of greater responsiveness to patient needs. It is much more enjoyable to respond to patients positively and in a timely fashion rather than having to explain and apologize why they can't meet patient expectations. In my experience, among healthcare workers, physicians experience the greatest gains in efficiency and quality of caring for their patients.

Before Lean, physicians often spent hours after clinics closed or hospital shifts ended, attending to patient requests and inquiries, filling out forms, filling prescriptions, and completing documentation. Very early after Lean implementations I began seeing physicians going home to their families within minutes after seeing their last patients. Despite leaving earlier, they were spending more time with their patients than ever before. Patient complaints went down and productivity increased. Done properly, Lean can fulfill the time-worn adage about doing more with less.

Early on we tried to do Lean implementations around the physicians so we didn't have to bother them. What a mistake! I now understand that you have to engage the physicians significantly in Lean implementations. This group, which gains so much from a Lean implementation, is highly motivated to see it continue and be sustainable. The book focuses on the necessary steps to engage physicians in a manner that will ensure their participation in the efforts to sustain Lean over time and provides physicians with information about how Lean might be implemented as well as some danger signs that could indicate that a plan is off course and, consequently, less likely to be as successful.

Perhaps larger multisite healthcare systems that have to continuously deploy Lean in several locations long after the consultants leave will derive the most value from this book. Maintaining the discipline of a standardized continuous deployment (spread) methodology is critical for large multisite organizations. All too often, after achieving great results in initial attempts in a clinic, ED, or hospital ward, senior leaders become very impatient and want to accelerate the changes for other parts of the organization. Because I have seen the negative results from trying to copy new work processes from one site to another and shortening implementation cycles, I've included a standardized implementation plan.

Early on I learned that there is quite a bit of variation in Lean approaches among institutions and consulting companies. The implementation plan in this book is based on the Shengo methodology, which I believe to be among the most comprehensive approaches to creating a Lean work environment. What distinguishes Shengo Lean from others is the added focus on operations (operators), regarding how people physically go about doing their work. More information is included in

Chapter 1. The book, however, is not intended to provide the technical knowledge and skills needed to conduct and sustain a Lean effort. An organization will require either external consultation or employed staff with the technical skills and certification to successfully deploy a Lean work system.

Notes

1. Technically, Lean is more encompassing than Toyota Production Systems; however, people often use the terms synonymously.

Foreword

This book intertwines two subjects near and dear to my heart: process efficiency and physician engagement. Both are critical to improving and maintaining the highest quality clinical outcomes

Healthcare professionals have always been committed to providing the best possible patient care. (I find most of them view what they do as a calling, not just a job.) But with Health Reform and pay-for-performance forcing our industry to provide better and better care with fewer and fewer dollars, the mission has taken on a new urgency. Organizations that can't improve their operations achieve and sustain measurably better clinical care may not be around for long.

That's why *Sustaining Lean in Healthcare: Developing and Engaging Physician Leadership* could not come at a better time.

We at Studer Group have always cared about process improvement. In fact, in our quest for the Malcolm Baldrige National Quality Award—which we gratefully received in 2010—we had to streamline and sharpen everything we do. It was a tough, yet deeply rewarding experience.

Our Baldrige journey truly helped us more deeply appreciate the value of efficiency and view its connection to exceptional quality with new eyes. And of course, it gave us new insights to share with to our partner organizations.

That said, we at Studer Group have always been advocates of Lean. During the past decade we've worked with more than 800 healthcare organizations, and we've seen over and over the benefits of improving productivity and saving time. When organizations cut waste—when they seek to zero in on the quickest, most direct, most effective way to do things—their efforts improve patient care and even save lives.

Of course, getting the processes right is only part of the picture. If an organization is to provide exceptional care consistently—every day, every department, every patient, every time—its entire foundation needs to be right.

That means all leaders at every level need to be aligned and working toward the same overarching goals.

Everyone needs to be following the right actions and behaviors—actions and behaviors that are proven to get results.

People need to be held accountable for their performance. (Objective evaluation systems, rather than the subjective ones many organizations use, help a lot here!)

Low performers need to be dealt with. Middle performers need to be coached and trained until they improve. High performers need to be rewarded and recognized.

At Studer Group, we help our partners install an operational framework—we call it Evidence-Based Leadership (EBL)—that helps them build this kind of organization. It reduces variances in leadership skills and processes so that every patient receives a consistent great experience.

Yes, when goals, behaviors and processes are aligned and working together, a healthcare organization is unstoppable. It's a great place for employees to work *and* for patients to receive care. And it's also the perfect environment in which to implement Lean improvements and maintain them over time.

I've seen it over and over: almost any organization can follow an improvement initiative and realize a short-term gain. But only one with a solid foundation can sustain these gains long term and get better year after year.

And that brings me to the other aspect of this book: physician engagement. Getting physicians fully integrated into your operations is critical—not only to sustain Lean improvements but also make sure every aspect of your operation is running smoothly.

The good news is that when your organization is built on a solid foundation, one that puts high quality patient care front and center, physicians will *want* to partner with you. They'll be active and enthusiastic participants in all of your improvement initiatives, whether it's Lean or something else.

Remember, in the hierarchy of physician needs, exceptional patient care comes first. And if you have what we at Studer Group call a "culture of always"—one that consistently generates predictable, positive outcomes—you won't have to convince physicians to join you in your quest to become more efficient. They'll already be on board.

I know you will benefit from *Sustaining Lean in Healthcare: Developing and Engaging Physician Leadership*. It's a practical, informative and ultimately inspiring book. But it's my hope that you won't stop there.

By making sure your entire organization is aligned and working together cohesively—not just your processes but your evaluation system, your leadership development, and your employee behaviors—your outcomes will just keep getter better and better and better. And I'm sure you'll agree that your patients deserve nothing less.

Quint Studer
Founder & CEO, Studer Group
2010 Malcolm Baldrige National Quality Award Recipient

Chapter 1

The Basics of Lean

Unfortunately, people use the term *Lean* to describe a variety of improvement activities. Process improvement work is often mistakenly called Lean; however, when used correctly, the term Lean refers to a specific set of tools and methods almost exclusively designed to rid the workplace of waste and inefficiency. For those of you who have recognized and been frustrated by the inefficiencies that constrain your ability to provide good patient care, Lean is the default tool to correct the problems you have identified. When combined with continuous improvement initiatives, it is an even more powerful tool to drive out waste.

Waste is categorized in similar ways across all industries. In Lean terms, waste has become known as The Eight Deadly Wastes. See Table 1.1. The reasons for eliminating waste include:

- At a time of healthcare reform and diminishing reimbursements, eliminating waste will be an important contributor to decreasing costs. While there are uncertainties about how to measure cost savings from Lean transformations and the associated reduction in waste, those savings clearly occur.
- Error reduction and improved patient safety.
- Reduced cycle times. Waiting times in physician offices, in emergency departments, and on hospital wards are clear patient dissatisfiers and a safety concern.
- Increased flow and throughput leading to increased productivity.
- Improved quality and reliability.
- Creating a more satisfying work experience.

While Lean does get rid of waste, the primary purpose is to add value for customers. Value added for a patient is defined by three criteria:

1. **The patient is physically or emotionally changed**. The patient's symptoms are relieved or perhaps he or she just needs reassurance. Even when patients are given an untreatable diagnosis, the clarification about what was wrong with them would qualify as an added value.
2. **The patient is willing to pay for it** (if he or she can). While the growing uninsured population in the United States is a major problem, this criterion assumes the patient would be

willing to pay either through health insurance premiums or direct payment (if they could) for the services received.

3. **It is done right the first time.** Repeating work steps to correct errors is very costly. The errors are not always apparent. I recently had $195 in unnecessary co-pays for medication because the sequencing of testing, office visit, results, and prescriptions were out of sync. Tests had to be repeated with consequent changes in medication before arriving at the correct drugs in the correct doses (Figure 1.1).

Lean had its origins in Japan with the birth of Toyota. In the 1940s, Taiichi Ohno and other leaders at Toyota began to develop and test many of the tools and techniques that were eventually recognized as the Toyota Production System (TPS). In 1956, a gentleman by the name of Shigeo Shingo drew Mr. Ohno's attention because of his teachings about the operator element in manufacturing. Mr. Shengo served as an external consultant to Toyota over the next several years, teaching process analysis, motion analysis, and time motion analysis. He also championed the idea that one needs to look at both the product and the operator separately. The primary product in healthcare is the medical care provided for the patient. The value derived from the care is judged through the eyes of the patient. There are also secondary products consisting of information and services

Table 1.1   Eight Deadly Wastes

Eight Deadly Wastes
1. Overproduction: Creating more material or service than is needed or sooner than it is needed. Examples include excess inventory than is needed and that needs to be stored somewhere. Another would be when preparing immunizations or other injections before they are needed and subsequently discarding them because there weren't as many patients as expected at a shot clinic.
2. Waiting: The term is self-explanatory and includes people, information, communications, and material. Waiting is so pervasive in healthcare that we even have rooms dedicated to the waste (e.g., waiting rooms).
3. Transportation: The movement of equipment, materials, paper, and communications by carrying or moving. Examples might be telephone messages written on message slips, attached to charts, and delivered to a clinical area. Another would be bringing shared thermometers or sphygmomanometers to an exam room.
4. Inventory: Unused inventory requires excessive space storage, expires, and hides other forms of waste from poorly functioning processes.
5. Motion: Any movement by people, including walking and reaching because needed equipment or material was not immediately available or proximate. The example with thermometers and sphygmomanometers above would also include motion waste.
6. Overprocessing: Doing more to a process or product than is required by a patient. Asking patients repeatedly for the same information in different steps of an office visit or hospital stay would be an example.
7. Errors: Errors cause repeat work and cause patient harm and, in the worst case, death.
8. Waste of talent: Created when frontline staff and physicians are not involved and accountable for the improvement process.

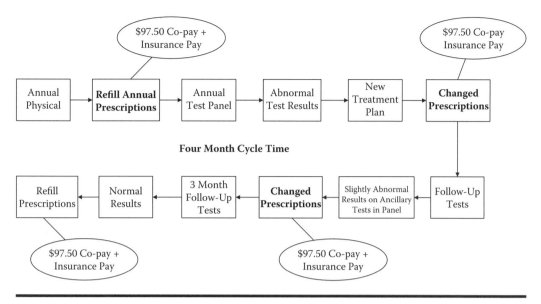

Figure 1.1   Unnecessary prescription refills.

such as prescription refills and responding to patient inquiries. The operators are the providers and clinicians who provide those services. Consequently, TPS has both a product-focused approach using certain tools and an operator-focused approach on work habits. Over time, through James Womack's influence, TPS[1] began to be replaced by the more generic term Lean. In fact, the Lean portfolio of tools and approaches is more inclusive than the original TPS.

In addition to product- and operator-focused approaches, the third foundational element in a successful and sustained Lean conversion is cultural (management) change. Lean cannot be sustained without this third element.

Generally, when people think of improvement projects they envision time-limited projects that have a clear start and end point. Any improvements gained during a project may or may not achieve long-term stability. Lean has a clear starting point but never ends. It begins with an implementation phase followed by a sustainment phase that is everlasting. In the following section, the various tools and approaches used with Lean are organized by implementation and sustainment phases (see Table 1.2); however, this is an artificial construct in that boundaries between the various categories are never black and white, and, in fact, all the elements can be used during both the implementation phase or sustainment phase. Perhaps the reader should simply interpret the table as showing where the different elements are used with greater emphasis. A brief description of these elements follows.

Implementation Phase

Lean Tools for Product and Process Approaches

Value Stream Maps (VSM)

Value stream maps (VSMs) are a foundational element of improvement work during a Lean implementation. They have clear starting and ending points and are designed to answer the following questions. They typically take 2–4 weeks to complete.

Table 1.2   Lean Tools in Implementation and Sustainment Phases

Implementation Phase	Sustainment Phase
Product-/Process-Focused Tools • Value Stream Maps • 6S • Kanban • Single Piece Flow • Level Loading (heijunka) • Product Process Flow	• Visual Controls • Huddles • Assessments (audits) • Gemba Walks • Culture/Management Change • Improvement Model (PDSA) • Kaizen Improvement Events
Operator-Focused Tools • Full Work Analysis (FWA) • Standard Work	

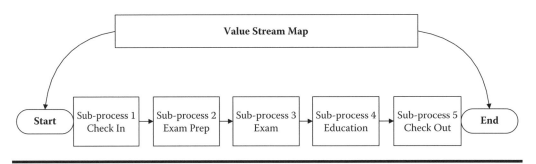

Figure 1.2   Value stream map.

VSM is an observational process to determine from a patient's perspective how much actual value-added time is included in their encounters with healthcare systems. VSM typically will include several individual processes that go together to complete a patient office visit. A process flow map (different from a value stream map) might be used to depict a simple process such as retrieving a medical record or preparing a patient for an exam or procedure. The value stream would include all those subprocesses (see Figure 1.2). VSMs should be done as an initial step in any Lean implementation. They might be for an office visit, an ED visit, an operation (either in- or outpatient), a hospital stay, food preparation in the hospital, or an admission process, among others.

Question typically answered during the mapping include:

■ What parts of our processes add value from our patient's and staff's perspectives?
■ What parts of our processes add cost?
■ What parts of our processes are unreliable and create variation?
■ What parts of our processes limit our capacity?
■ What parts of our processes reduce our flexibility?
■ What parts of our processes do we need to change to eliminate, simplify, or combine to improve or reduce our cycle times?

Table 1.3   Value-Added versus Non-Value-Added Time in an Office Visit

Value-Added Activity	Non-Value-Added Activity
• Time spent with the physician • Time spent getting education and advice • Post-visit instructions for care	• Multiple attempts to get someone to answer the phone • Hand-off and hold time when trying to schedule an appointment • Wait time until appointment actually occurs • Repetitively being asked the reason for a visit by different staff (and physicians) • Waiting in the lobby and examination room • Waiting for personnel to complete regulatory documents • Waiting for clinical information that is not available at a visit • Waiting for staff to find handouts, equipment for procedures, etc.

Don Berwick, MD, and others in healthcare have suggested that there may be as much as 30%–40% waste in healthcare; however, there is an even greater amount of non-value-added activity that interferes with our efficiencies and ability to provide real value to patients. There are three main categories of activity in the value stream:

1. Value-added activity (patient and staff perspective).
2. Required non-value-added activity (required waste) (HIPPA, Medicare statements, reporting requirements, etc.)—the list is long. We all decry the multitude of requirements and paperwork that must be completed in order to care for patients; however, in my experience, it is often how we choose to go about meeting the requirements that creates more waste, rather than the actual requirement.
3. Non-value-added activity.

In all the value streams I've been involved in mapping, the percentage of value-added time is less than 5%–20% of the total time spent by the patient to receive care. Conversely, 80%–95% of the time spent by patients receiving care is what they often consider a waste of time. During a value stream mapping, there are typically debates about whether something is value added or not; however, one only has to imagine the list of activities that are typically required in an office visit to recognize non-value added time. See Table 1.3.

During a typical Lean implementation, the value stream is initially mapped in its current state.

Current state value stream map: A current state value stream map is constructed using direct observation of patients, products, or staff involved in the care process. It should never be constructed in a meeting room based only on people's recollections of the process. Typically, several patients can be observed and the results (time) for each step averaged (include a hi–low range if there is wide variation). (See Figure 1.3.) All of the steps in the process are then laid out into the value stream map. The value stream map combines all elements of the value stream being observed, product (patient), material, communication, inventory, etc. Value stream maps give you a very good snapshot of what is taking place in the system.

Elements of a current state value stream map include:

■ The steps in the process
■ The amount of time required for each step (cycle time) as well as the entire value stream (total throughput time)

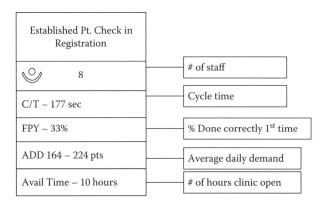

Figure 1.3 Value stream map data box.

- Wait times (storage of people, materials, equipment, etc.) between process steps
- Number of staff available
- Value-added and non-value-added results
- First pass yield (FPY): Time the product or process is correct the first time through that step
- Communication requirements required to complete the process (electronic, telephonic, and in person)

Value stream maps can be very detailed, large documents that are difficult to illustrate on a single page. There are numerous books and websites dedicated to VSM.

Future state value stream maps: Once the current state VSM is completed, the results are reviewed to determine opportunities for improvement. Depending on the size of the value stream, it is not unusual to generate 50–60 ideas. These are subsequently prioritized to determine their sequence for testing. The ideas are added to the current state map to show the work that will be completed in the next few months, and the VSM is labeled as a future state map.

Ideal state value stream map: At some point during an implementation, an ideal state VSM will be created. This ideal should represent what kind of improvement might be achieved in 3–5 years. It is used to stay focused on long-range goals and is created through a brainstorming process.

6S

6S is a methodology used to ensure that everything we use in a process has a place and everything is in its place. In some settings, the term 5S is used. The sixth S is for safety. There is not an industrywide standard to use either 5S or 6S. In healthcare it makes sense to add the "Safety" component. The goals of doing 6S are multiple. One is to remove the clutter in our work areas that interferes with our ability to see and recognize problems inherent in a given process. 6S also leads to decreased motion waste: having to look for supplies and equipment. In my experience, when observing and timing, temporary clinical and clerical staff take a minimum of twice as long to complete a given task compared to their permanent peers. That might not be surprising, but when combined with other tools such as standard work (see below), 6S can make the time gap disappear.

Sort: The process of going through everything in the workplace and setting aside rarely or infrequently used or outdated items. After a short period of time (determined by the circumstance at the work station), if they haven't been used, remove them from the workplace. During the time that infrequently used items are set aside, they are kept in a location nearby in case they are needed. Time frames for determining whether to keep or discard an item from the workplace can range from 1 to 3 months.

Set in Order: Determine the ideal locations for equipment, supplies, medications, etc. Locations are based on accessibility and frequency of use. The locations are then labeled; in some cases, shadow box outlines are created with tape so that everyone knows where the item should go once they are done using it.

Standardize: Standardize what was decided in the *Set in Order* phase to all common work areas. There is often a good deal of resistance from staff and managers to instituting the Set in Order and Standardize components. Employees often have personal mementoes in their work area. Depending on the size of the work area or desktop, a dedicated area with standardized size and content can be used to overcome the resistance.

Managers and leaders who have offices that aren't shared are highly resistant to this approach. Not only should they 6S their offices to serve as role models, but they also will find that their work efficiency will improve. When I initially performed 6S in my office (see Figure 1.4), I was motivated to be a role model; however, I was pleasantly surprised when my work efficiency significantly improved. I hadn't realized how much time I spent looking for things and how much unnecessary clutter was in my office.

Shine: Keep the work area clean and free of clutter.

Sustain: Create an ongoing audit of the work area to ensure the changes are maintained. Initially, regular audits (at least weekly) should be conducted by immediate supervisors; however, the ultimate goal would be to have employees do their own audits on the workplace.

Safety: Survey the work area for possible safety hazards (e.g., potential sources of tripping, items falling, exposure to toxins, shock, etc.) Figures 1.5a and 1.5b show "before" and "after" examples of 6S. In the "after" picture, all containers are standardized and color-coded for expiration dates.

Figure 1.4   6S on individual desktop.

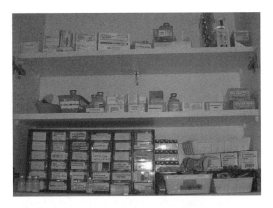

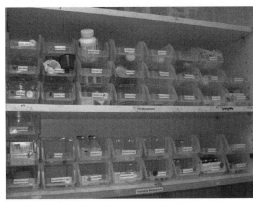

Figure 1.5 (a) Medication cabinet before, (b) Medication cabinet after.

Kanban

Kanban is the Japanese term for signboard. In this case, the "signboard" is usually some sort of card/container for the supplies at the point of use. The card contains key information about how much of a particular item is needed to replace current supplies and an indication of when to order those supplies. Kanban systems should be used for virtually anything that needs replacement or recycling. The range of items is quite large and includes small items such as tongue blades or a piece of educational literature to surgical instruments that need to be sterilized. The overall design is to pull supplies to the right place in the right amount at the right time. The end result for physicians and staff is that they should never have to wait or look for tools or supplies in order to complete a current task.

Single Piece Flow

Healthcare, in general, tends to be a batch-and-queue industry. We batch patients in waiting rooms and have stacks of charts piled on our desks with their attached refill requests, patient inquiries, and dictations. For those physicians in ambulatory and inpatient care, it is common to receive batches of refill requests and patient inquiries in bursts, typically at the end of a morning or afternoon session in the clinic or at the end of shift work in the hospital. Physicians contribute to batching when they wait until the end of a session or shift to complete their documentation or by holding on to charts while they wait for results or dictations to come back to them.

In one clinic medical record department, charts were typically batched and held until the chart cart was full (usually 40–50 charts) delivered 2–3 times a day. During the Lean implementation, we asked the medical records staff to start delivering requested charts every 15 minutes. Of course, that created an outpouring of protests because they could barely get their work done as it was. In their minds, only disaster could follow.

Nonetheless, we followed the ground rules previously set to try everything, measure the results, and subsequently decide whether to continue the change, modify the change, or abandon it. The results were startling. Not only did physicians start going home earlier (their patient requests were evenly spaced throughout the day), but the medical records staff also had extra time on their hands. Can you guess what happened? The medical records staff never realized how much time they were spending on repeated requests from patients or staff in the clinical areas because of not receiving timely responses. In addition, when they were batching, you can be sure the clinic staff and physicians were batching. Consequently, large stacks of charts were scattered around the clinic. The staff spent large amounts of time looking for those charts. I once watched a staff person go through a clinic five consecutive times looking for a chart hidden in a pile I was observing. In that case, the team was doing what is called a product process flow (see below). The analysis is carried out to see what happens with medical records, messages, and requests over the course of a day.

The medical records staff was able to catch up on loose filing, chart file backs, and organization of the work area. They turned from being severe skeptics to ardent supporters. They openly shared how much they hated coming to work prior to the change because everyone was always giving them a hard time to feeling like "it was a fairy tale" and work was once again fun.

A Simple Exercise

This exercise is designed to demonstrate the difference between batch and queue and single piece flow.

Gather a group of 5–7 people around a table. Have one serve as a timekeeper.

1st step: Take 10 pennies, and arrange them all either with heads or tails (not both) showing on a table. Arrange participants around the table either in a straight line or around the table. Each worker's task is to turn all the pennies over to the other side, and *then and only then* pass them to the next person in line to do the same thing. Turn the pennies, then pass them down the line. The timer starts timing when the first penny is turned over until the last person in line turns over the last penny. Record the time.

2nd step: Repeat the exercise, but this time pass the pennies down one at a time as soon as they are turned over. *Do not* wait until all the pennies in the individual's batch are turned. Record the time.

3rd step: Discuss the differences between the two methods, and record your observations. It should become immediately apparent why single piece flow is more efficient and timely.

Typical observations include the fact that people in the later stages of the process are wasting time waiting for the pennies to arrive in the first phase of the experiment. A facilitator should then ask for examples in the work area where materials are handled the same way. Typical examples include prescription requests, messages, lab requests, appointment requests, and other inquiries. Changing to Just In Time (JIT) handling of materials and tasks as in the second method is a tremendous time saver.

Level Loading (*Heijunka*)

Heijunka is a Japanese term that refers to leveling the demand for production evenly throughout any designated period of time (hour, day, week, etc.). At first glance, that might seem impossible in healthcare; however, when you analyze scheduled and urgent or emergent demand, some interesting patterns emerge. When analyzing scheduled and emergency operating room (OR) cases, emergency demand is often less variable than scheduled cases by day of the week. In one hospital, the Intensive Care Unit predictably filled up in the middle of the week on Wednesdays. What followed was a logjam in throughput (flow) of patients through the hospital. Patients waited for extended periods of time in the Post Anesthesia Care Unit (PACU) and the ED for a bed in the ICU. Transfers to step-down units and general wards slowed, length of stay went up, and patients' care was extended into the weekends when fewer services were available. The cycle would repeat itself the following week. Of course, there were no predictable increases in emergencies on Wednesdays. The problem was created by the scheduling of surgeons whose patients had increased use of the ICU (cardiovascular, thoracic, etc.) for postoperative care. The scheduling was, in part, created by the surgeons' preferences for which days of the week they wanted to be in the office versus the operating room. The demand in this case could be leveled by negotiating different OR days and office days among the surgical subspecialists who generated postoperative care in the ICU to smooth the flow and spread the ICU cases out during the week.

In the process of doing Advanced Access for a few years, it was once again apparent that the clinic scheduling process was creating a good portion of the variation in demand. In primary care clinics, the demand is typically greatest on Mondays and trails off by Fridays. Ironically, the clinics had the highest amount of patients scheduled on Mondays and the fewest on Fridays. So demand was highest on the days when the clinic was least able to meet patient needs (see Figure 1.6).

How would this happen? When physicians told their patients they wanted to see them in two weeks (or any time interval), patients took them very literally. The patient would present at the front desk and insist on an appointment in two weeks on the same day of the week. It was a self-fulfilling process that created the scenario depicted in Figure 1.6. By working with the staff and physicians and doing some scripting (e.g., physician script = "I want to see you in *about* two

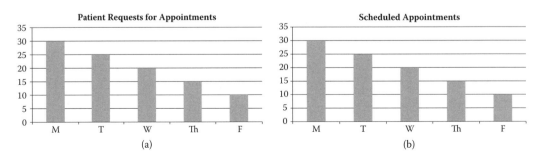

Figure 1.6 Traditional scheduling scenario by day of week.

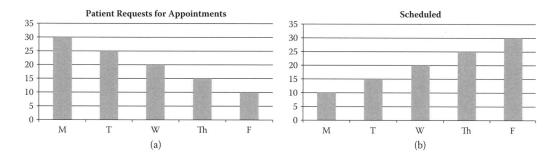

Figure 1.7 Scheduling scenario after scripting changes.

weeks, *the receptionist will help decide which day works best*") allowed the clinic to shift scheduled demand to better accommodate same-day demand in the future. Then the scheduling profile looked like that depicted in Figure 1.7. Now prebooked appointments took up a smaller percentage of the day when patients typically have more demand for appointments. Schedulers were better able to respond to patient requests for timely appointments. The same patterns were present in specialty offices; they were just different days of the week, depending on when the physicians were in the hospital.

Product Process Flow

Product Process Flow (PPF) is the observational work already described in part in the section on VSM. Detailed analysis of the medical care product (through observing and recording the patient experience), service products (observation of refill request through completion of the prescription), and information (observation of the medical chart as it is handled by various individuals in a practice or hospital setting) is followed by analysis value-added/non-value-added steps as well as waste categories.

Lean Tools for Operator-Focused Approaches

Full Work Analysis

Full Work Analysis (FWA) is a detailed second-by-second review of a segment of an individual's work day. Clerical and clinical staff and physicians are videotaped for about 30 minutes of work. Times should be selected representing a roughly average workload (neither too busy nor too slow). Once the tape is completed, a session will be scheduled for a period of 1–2 hours for the individual to sit down with the team to review the tape. Using a stopwatch, every second of the tape is analyzed for different types of waste. The tape is broken down into categories of whether or not the step is work relative to value added for the patient. Representative categories include value-added, non-value-added but required, pure waste (idle time), travel, inspection, etc. The purpose of FWA is not to determine how hard a person is working; it is not a statistically significant sampling that could be used for that purpose. Rather, it is to see how an individual is working and, together with the individual and the team, identify activities that are wasteful and, therefore, competing for time that could be spent adding value for the patient.

Initially, there is a natural hesitation and reluctance to agree to being videotaped. Once assurances are provided about keeping the distribution of the tapes between the team and the individual as well as promises that it will not affect their employability, most employees are willing to be taped. As a general rule, people like the review process. It is not uncommon to hear people comment that they had never seen themselves work before and that they actually enjoyed the experience.

Standard Work

Standard work is a process of collecting information from the frontline workers about the steps they take to do their job. Those individuals are then tasked through a consensus process with defining the best way to do the work. Standard work should not be confused with policy and procedure manuals that often, once written, gather dust on a bookshelf. Standard work is a single sheet of paper with brief descriptions of the steps documented (see Figure 1.8).

A standardized worksheet normally lists the work elements (steps), key points about the step, and why it is important as well as the time required to complete the step. These sheets are posted in prominent places at the various workstations. Standard work should be completed for all levels in the organization, including senior management. They are valuable tools in two ways. When temporary or permanent staff members unfamiliar with the work process are called to duty, they can anticipate and actively engage in the work process without having to stand around waiting for someone to give them directions for the work.

An ED physician recently communicated how valuable standard work was for him when the nurse he was working with decided to work in her own way. It was interfering with his ability to see and care for patients. Having a documented standard work reference allowed him to quickly ask the nurse to carry out the standard work. When that did not happen, he went to the supervisor to get compliance on the part of that nurse or to find another one. Afterward, they were able to hold a debriefing on why it was important to perform the standard work and inquire why it was difficult to perform. The nonjudgmental debriefing is an important step in improving standard work.

Sustainment Phase

Visual Controls

Visual controls are visible indicators for how well a process is working. A well-known example is the tracking board in airport terminals. Passengers are kept informed about flight times, cancellations, and delays. Imagine walking into a clinic or ED where there is prominent visual information (the equivalent of an airport tracking board) that shows whether your doctor is on time, delayed, or even worse, canceled for the day. This is an example of a high-tech electronic visual control; however, for the most part visual controls are best developed and kept current through manual updates by the frontline staff. You don't often find visual controls in a computer, nor is it necessarily desirable to create electronic visual controls.

Visual controls are designed in a way that allows staff and managers to know how well a process is performing in as close to real time as possible. For instance, a Post Anesthesia Care Unit (PACU) might want to monitor its pace during the day. By using an hour-by-day chart, everyone would know what sort of pace they were on. The chart is constructed by determining the number of patients scheduled for surgery for the day divided by the hours of the day. Discharges per hour should match the number of patients expected per hour, once surgery

STANDARD WORK		Job Function: Charge Posting	Date: July 28, 2008
		Area: Charge Poster location	Prepared By
		Operation Name: Charge Poster	Approved By
			Update Name

	Work Elements / Important Steps	Est. Time	Key Points	Reasons for Key Points	Sketch/Drawing/Picture
1	Charge poster to pick up superbills from designated areas.	5m			
2	Sorts charge tickets into manageable batches by provider/department. Checks to see if all information on charge ticket is correct to post.	10m	Smooths workflow		
3	Buck sheet management.	1m	Charge poster to attach buck sheet to charge ticket and give to provider indicating what is missing.	Missed charges accuracy	
4	Work queue.	30m	Understand how to use the work queue with an explanation of what is missing and also how to work the work queue.	incomplete or inaccurate charges won't go through	
5	Charge poster to resolve incomplete encounter forms with providers as soon as convenient but at least daily.	30m	Bring to providers attention as early in the day as possible	Corrections won't be delayed a day	
6	Missing ticket process. Runs missing ticket report daily after they have posted the batch.	45m	Works Missing ticket report until it is clean Charge poster to review missing ticket report with supervisor once daily to determine problem areas.	Lost income Every patient must have a charge	
7	Charge poster to run missing ticket report 2xday				
8	Understand what an ABN is. Understand modifiers GA,GZ, etc. Understands ICD-9 and CPT				
9					
10					
11	Total Estimated Time	121m			

Charge poster #1 Charge Poster 2 & 3

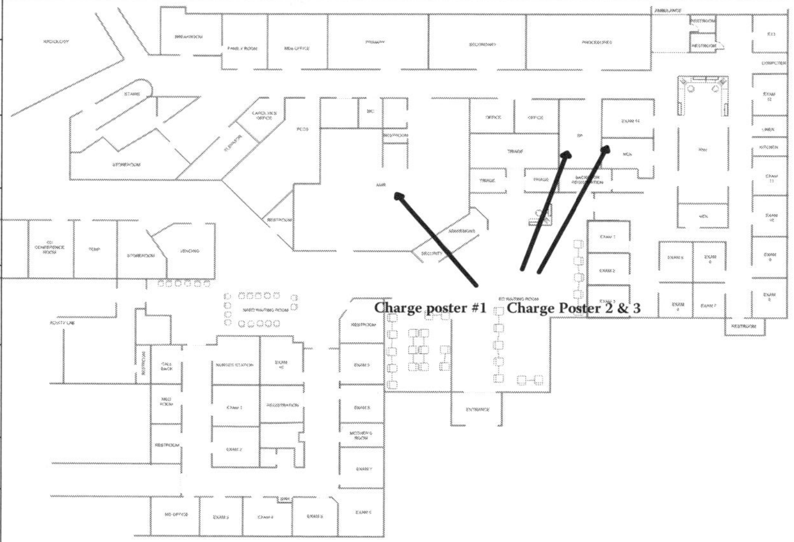

Figure 1.8 Charge poster standard work.

PACU Flow ideal												
Time	7:00 AM	8:00 AM	9:00 AM	10:00 AM	11:00 AM	12:00 PM	1:00 PM	2:00 PM	3:00 PM	4:00 PM	5:00 PM	6:00 PM
Scheduled in	0	1	3	3	4	4	2	1	1			
Actual discharge			1	2	3	4	3	3	2			
Gap			−2	−3	−4	−4	−3	−1	0			

Figure 1.9 Hour-by-day report for PACU—normal flow.

PACU Flow Delays												
Time	7:00 AM	8:00 AM	9:00 AM	10:00 AM	11:00 AM	12:00 PM	1:00 PM	2:00 PM	3:00 PM	4:00 PM	5:00 PM	6:00 PM
Scheduled in	0	1	3	3	4	4	2	1	1	0	0	0
Actual discharge			1	1	2	3	2	1	1	2	2	1
Gap			−2	−4	−6	−7	−7	−7	−7	−5	−3	−2

Figure 1.10 Hour-by-day report for PACU—delayed flow.

patients start arriving. On a normal day, the hour-by-day chart posted on the white board might look like Figure 1.9. Staff expects the peak number of patients being discharged to occur at midday and to be normally behind by 3–4 patients in the late morning. They would anticipate a normal day.

On some days, discharges are delayed (see Figure 1.10). In the past, the staff usually started looking for solutions by mid- to late afternoon. It is too late to effectively mitigate the delays at that point. By 10 a.m., suspicion should be raised and the next hour closely monitored. Intervention at this point would include a brief 5-minute huddle to determine root causes (e.g., bed availability in ICU or surgical unit, acuity of patients, staffing issues, lack of timely transport). At this point, attempts would be made to resolve the problems or, at the least, to institute contingency plans.

In another example, telephone operators (schedulers) in a clinic were routinely only able to answer 50%–60% of phone calls within one minute. Consequently, abandonment rates were as high as 25%. For years, electronic data of monthly telephone stats were reviewed by management and various fixes attempted. None were successful. During the Lean implementation, staff members were asked to track their time available (time spent answering the phone instead of breaks, lunches, brief timeouts, etc.). They used daily electronic data and were asked to post the results in their work area. In addition, they were to track calls answered in one minute and the abandonment rate. A blank graph was printed and posted in their work area (see Figure 1.11). While the staff thought they were available the majority of the time, the data showed average availability at 40%–50%. Once the staff started monitoring their own work, the percent available rose and the percentage of calls answered in one minute rose to 90% or greater in just 5 days.

A month later all of us were feeling a little guilty about using this visual control and took the graph down and stopped the practice of having the staff track the data. We were concerned about

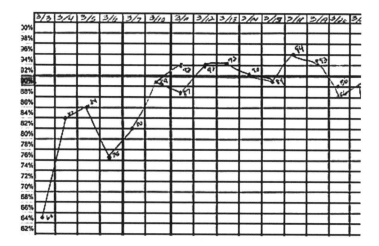

Figure 1.11 Percentage of telephone calls answered within 1 minute.

it being too judgmental or punitive. The results almost immediately dropped back to the old patterns. The staff asked to reinstate the visual controls and their accountability to record the data. They indicated they used it like a metronome or speedometer, and they had a better sense of how the process was working.

Huddles

Huddles are stand-up sessions at the start of each day or shift. They are attended by members of the care team as appropriate for the setting. In the hospital, huddles are the equivalent of rounding with the team, which might include physicians, nurses, care coordinators (discharge planners), pharmacists, respiratory therapists, etc. In the clinic, the team might consist of a physician, nurse, clerk, medical records staff, etc.

Huddles should always be conducted with everyone standing. When people sit, it too often turns into a meeting. They should last no longer than 5–7 minutes. The purpose of huddles is to anticipate the work of the day. What will be happening to the patients that day? Are they prepared? Is the necessary lab and x-ray work available? In the clinic, the schedule would be reviewed to anticipate patient needs, identify unnecessary appointments (routine follow-up from an urgent care or ED visit which might be handled with a phone call), and identify times of day when, if necessary, extra patients could be added to the schedule.

An additional component of huddles might include updates on various improvement projects, including status of the project as well as results obtained. Perhaps changes to the improvement project could be discussed as well.

Assessment (Audits)

The term *audit*, while widely used in Lean manufacturing, carries with it a negative connotation that is punitive and judgmental. Others have used the term *rounding*. Rounding is too easily confused with the concept of leadership rounding, which often has a predetermined script and set of questions or instructions. I prefer the term *assessment.* According to the Merriam-Webster dictionary, *assess* probably derives from medieval Latin *assessus,* which means to sit beside or assist in the office of a judge. In reality, assessments ought to be partnerships in learning and improving a process.

In a pre-Lean organization, process changes are often made without any real-time monitoring of the results. If any monitoring is done at all, it is typically in some form of electronic format collected and reviewed on a monthly or quarterly basis. Furthermore, these reports are almost exclusively regarding the results rather than reporting on the functioning of the process itself. One of the key success factors for sustaining Lean lies in meaningful implementation of frequent assessments of a process or use of Lean tools, published in highly visible locations in the work area.

What should be assessed on a regular basis? The answer will vary from organization to organization and department to department; however, there are some shared standard assessments common to all. Assessments about how well standard work is being carried out and the status of 6S would be two such examples. Visual controls can be an adjunct to assessments in that they provide a snapshot in time about how a given process is working; however, visual controls can create a false sense of security if they are conducted without also performing assessments that are more sensitive to identifying problems before outcomes are impacted.

Who should perform the assessments? Typically, a hierarchy is used in which the responsibility for performing the assessment falls on an individual's supervisor. Ideally, individuals and teams doing frontline work will eventually perform their own self-assessments, turning to their supervisor only when there are problems they cannot resolve. Creation of standard work and regular assessments on performance should extend all the way to the CEO.

When should assessments be completed? Frontline work and tools should be assessed on a daily or weekly basis. That is relatively easy to do for leads and supervisors. The higher the person in the organizational hierarchy, the less frequently assessments are performed; senior vice presidents probably cannot perform assessments more often than quarterly.

How should assessments be performed? When assessments indicate everything is as it should be, then use of customary rewards and recognitions is appropriate. When assessments show deficiencies or gaps, the process should be performed in an exploratory learning manner. They are not meant to catch someone not doing his or her job, or to be punitive. The moment that happens, employees will begin trying to hide things or downplay process malfunctions. A first step is often to have the involved staff or employees make the first comments toward identifying the problem while performing the assessment. The idea is to teach them to be proficient in performing them. Supervisors and others can then offer their opinions and discuss ideas with the staff. If gaps are identified, a collaborative problem-solving approach should be used. The 6S Checklist Assessment in Figure 1.12 is an example of a tool that can be used during the assessment. As with visual controls, simply completing a checklist and filing it away falls far short of the purpose of performing the assessments. They should be used to help reach a state of continuous improvement and support for staff.

Regular assessments along with *gemba* walks and visual controls are a foundational cornerstone in sustaining Lean efforts after the consultants are long gone.

Gemba Walks

Gemba refers to the place where work is done (the front line). Gemba walks are another foundational element in sustaining a Lean environment. Senior leaders down through supervisors should have regularly scheduled walks. Unlike leadership rounds, where there are often scripted questions

Date: _____

Auditor: _____

Department: _____

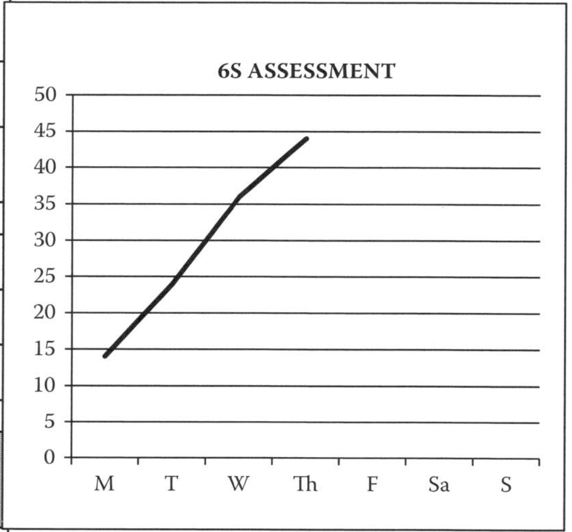

6S ASSESSMENT

6S Checklist Assessment	M	T	W	Th	F	Sa	S
Are nonproductive items removed form the work areas? (magazines, food, cell phones, etc.)	1	2	3	3			
Are work areas clean? (clean surfaces and monitors; trash & recycle bins emptied daily)	3	3	3	3			
Are needed items in the work areas stored safely and within easy reach? (cords bundled, no boxes on floor, drawers and cabinet doors closed)	2	1	2	2			
Are visual controls and indicators established and marked?	0	0	1	2			
Is there overall evidence of Continuous Improvement for the process and system?	0	1	2	3			
Is an agreed upon 6S layout posted in the work area?	3	3	3	3			
Is desk/countertop taped to show location of standard items?	0	0	1	2			
Is work area free of personal items except for those items approved and appropriately located?	0	2	3	3			
Are cabinets and drawers in work area organized with agreed upon quantity and item location?	1	2	2	2			
Are cabinets and drawers labeled	0	1	2	3			
Total:	10	15	22	26	0	0	0

Scoring: 0 = No Evidence; 1 = Early Incomplete Effort;
2 = Mostly Complete in All Areas;
3 = Complete in All Areas

	M	T	W	Th	F	Sa	S
Day Total	14	24	36	44			

Figure 1.12   6S assessment tool.

and comments, gemba walks are a learning place, a place for you to see with your own eyes what is happening. By quietly observing the process or reviewing visual controls, you should be able to get a sense of how a process is working. In addition, asking employees about how the process is working is another learning avenue. But leaders should be there to teach as well. They should be teaching others about Lean thinking. The implication is, of course, that leaders need to be well versed in Lean knowledge. Gemba walks should be occurring on a weekly basis by someone in a leadership position. They may or may not include assessment work but a review of others' regular assessment reports, and asking staff about problems and how they go about solving problems should all be in the portfolio of inquiry.

Culture Change

Successful implementation of the four foundational elements for sustaining a Lean effort includes:

1. Leader standard work
2. Visual controls
3. Daily accountability process (i.e., assessments)
4. Leadership discipline[2]

The combination should create a profound culture change. I really like David Mann's definition of culture from his book *Creating a Lean Culture*. For some, culture is a very nebulous term. For David, culture is "the sum of peoples' habits related to how they get their work done." Fundamentally, Lean is about changing how we work. Therefore, there has to be a change in culture. David goes on to say "a company's culture is a result of its management system. … culture is critical, and to change it, you have to change your management system."[2]

Most managers and leaders in healthcare have been trained in traditional management approaches that were taught (and still are) in business management schools. Or they've come up through the ranks and had no management training. Managers in a Lean environment require a different skill set, attitude, and approach (see Table 1.4).

I believe healthcare culture in general poses an even greater challenge. Those of us who are in healthcare want to help people. We are healers and fixers. The balance of pride and self-esteem in our work heavily favors rescuing people from death and disease over prevention. When we have a problem at work, we are genetically wired to step in and fix it and move on to the next problem. These quick fixes and work-arounds eventually catch up with us by making processes more and more complex without solving the underlying root cause.

The staff of a Pediatric Intensive Care Unit (PICU) process-mapped what it took to give a single oral dose of medicine in their unit. One might expect the process to be a bit more complicated than other areas of the hospital because their patients have serious life-threatening illness or trauma; however, everyone was shocked when we learned that it took 54 separate steps (all of which could be failure points in the process) to give a child one dose of an oral antibiotic. Through historical knowledge of the staff and other analysis, you could see why the process had become more complex; for example, there had been an episode when a nurse prepared a wrong dose from a stock bottle, which led to unit dosing, and delayed doses led to tighter controls on ordering. Each was a work-around designed to fix a problem that occurred in the past. The result was a complex process with many opportunities for errors.

Table 1.4 Modern versus Lean Management in Healthcare

Modern Management	Lean Management
Strong focus on vertical functions and departments in the organization for control	Strong focus on horizontal (patient) flow across departments and organizations
Managerial *authority* granted by senior leaders of departments and business units	Managerial responsibility granted by next higher manager to solve cross-functional, horizontal (patient flow) problems
Line managers judged on their departmental results (increasingly, financial)	Line managers judged on the state of their process with rapid feedback loops from next-level managers **"If the process is right, the results will be right"***
Top-down direction Managers make decisions with a compliance focus Make the target or explain the variances	Planning and direction in circular feedback loops with bosses asking: • What do you think our problem is? • What are potential countermeasures? • How do we test with PDSA? "Planning is invaluable but plans rapidly become worthless, so why explain variances rather than propose new countermeasures?"
Decisions made by managers far from the point of value creation, by analyzing data in a meeting room	Decisions made at the point of value creation, by converting data into facts. (Go see, ask why, show respect)
Problem solving and improvement conducted by analysts and quality departments	Problem solving and improvement conducted by frontline managers with cross-functional teams
Standardization of activities conducted by leaders and managers with little frontline interaction and little auditing	Standardization of activities conducted by line managers in collaboration with work teams with frequent assessments
"Go fast" and "jump to solutions" as a general mandate	"Go slow" general mandate. Start with the problem, and pursue many potential countermeasures in parallel

Source: Adapted with permission from James Womack on Lean Management Video from the Lean Enterprise Institute.

How often have you heard senior leaders say, "Don't bring me a problem unless you have a solution"? Managers are often thinking the same thing. Instead, we should be embracing the discovery and perceiving it as an opportunity to learn and improve. Rather than looking immediately for solutions, we should be seeking to understand the problem (and why it is a problem) and working with frontline staff to identify possible countermeasures for testing in repeatable Improvement Model (PDSA) cycles (See Figure 1.11). Unfortunately, in many healthcare organizations, managers

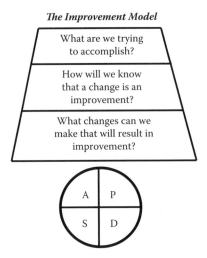

Figure 1.13   The Improvement Model. (From The Improvement Guide, Langley Nolan et al., 1996.)

are rewarded for quick fixes and solutions. Managers I have worked with complain about always having to "put out fires" but quickly smile and say "thank you" when they are recognized in meetings for handling yet another crisis.

Managers in a Lean environment must have a deep knowledge of process management and improvement. They need to be skillful in the use of quality improvement tools such as root cause analysis. They must be good facilitators and teachers and understand various methodologies to apply the skills and tools. Use of the Improvement Model for continuous improvement for simple problem solving or improving a stable process should be second nature and used at least weekly, if not daily. Experience and knowledge in running *kaizen* (Japanese term for "good change") events is another part of the manager portfolio that is important for long-term success. *Kaizen* events are 1–5-day problem-solving or improvement (when a stable process needs to improve) gatherings of cross-functional teams. They are generally characterized as having a process mapping phase, brainstorming countermeasures or improvement ideas, testing the ideas and, finally, developing a plan to implement the changes agreed upon immediately in the work area. *Kaizen* events might be run by someone from a quality department, but managers need to know when to request an event for improvement.

Improvement Model

> Don't be too timid or squeamish about your actions. All life is an experiment. The more experiments you make, the better.

Ralph Waldo Emerson

The Improvement Model was first proposed by Gerald Langley and Tom Nolan and colleagues in their 1996 book, *The Improvement Guide—A Practical Approach to Enhancing Organizational Performance.*[3] It is a practical approach to improvement that involves answering three questions and testing ideas in a defined, standard manner (Plan, Do, Study, Act [PDSA]). The model is very similar to the scientific method and the clinical decision-making process.

The first step in any improvement process is to answer the following three questions.

What Are We Trying to Accomplish?

This question is foundational in improvement work. "What is the problem?" is another way of phrasing the question. It is also common to have a team come together with entirely different mental models (our view of the world based on our life experiences) of the problem to be addressed or what they are trying to accomplish. I routinely ask this question now in meetings and continue to be surprised at the awkward silence that follows. It often takes some time to work through to a consensus regarding the real nature of the problem and what needs to be accomplished.

Note that the question is not about identifying solutions. Solutions should not be identified until the true nature of the problem and desired state or goal is determined. When trying to answer this question, improvement tools such as root cause analysis may be used to determine the answer. The answer should be concise (usually less than 25 words) and should include a goal or target. Setting goals or targets is important in order to have shared criteria to judge success. How often have you participated in an improvement project and at the end discover that people have different perceptions about the success of the project? In short, the answer should be clear, descriptive, and measurable—but not encyclopedic.

How Will We Know That a Change Is an Improvement?

Every improvement cycle must have definable measures. During small change cycle improvement, work process measures will often predominate. At times, it is difficult to define outcome measures that are timely enough to validate that the changes are an improvement. Patient satisfaction data are frequently gathered on a monthly basis. In order to be helpful, improvement measures should be as close to real time as possible. An outcome measure of patient satisfaction might not be timely enough to judge success about changes made to improve the patient experience. If a team decided to end every patient encounter with a phrase such as "have I met all your needs?" they might choose a process measure that reflects how often the staff asked the question. Process measures should reflect that the defined process is functioning as designed. Outcome measures reflect the desired product or desired health status of a patient.

What Changes Can We Make That Will Result in an Improvement?

Have you ever been on a team with individuals who lobbied interminably for the perfect solution? The beauty of small cycle improvement work is that whatever change you make will be measured and studied to determine whether it worked. This allows the introduction of the term "right enough." In small cycle improvement work, failure is usually inconsequential, so the cost of doing it wrong is mitigated. So it is easier to reach a consensus about an approach that is under consideration. Changes to test may be identified through brainstorming and prioritization before moving into the testing or PDSA phase of the Improvement Model.

The Plan, Do, Study, Act (PDSA) cycle has been an important tool to engage physicians in this work. To treat a patient and not follow up on the patient's status for months either through testing, telephonic, or electronic outreach, or patient self-reporting would be anathema to physicians.

Yet, in our attempts to improve the health of a process, we traditionally make changes and never check to see how the changes are working for months at a time. This creates the potential for a lot of damage to be caused before it is discovered that it was not a good change. I've found that physicians are more willing to go along with or participate in changes as long as they are assured that the impact of the change will be measured and they will participate in the Study phase (see below) of the experiment. In one case, we had an opportunity to try a makeshift electronic order entry process to replace physicians completing multiple forms to order lab, x-ray, and cardiac testing. At least one physician in the group was adamant that the change would be a disaster. When informed that the impact on their work time would be monitored daily and a decision made within a week, the individual went along with the experiment. The change was acceptable for physicians who were very proficient with computers; however, anyone who wasn't very proficient suffered through lots of frustration and lost time trying to use the process. It was clear that it was not the right solution, and it was stopped after two days. From then on, they were willing to try any improvement ideas.

What follows is a description of each phase of the PDSA cycle.

Plan

During the Plan phase, the steps necessary to implement the change are identified and sequenced. The plan may include training, and developing methodology to measure the outcomes as well as day-to-day monitoring. In the case of the order entry example above, some technical support was necessary as well as a 30-minute training session for the physicians. In the meantime, baseline measurements were collected on how long it took physicians to complete necessary order forms in the current situation.

It is important to note that the Plan should include only what you can *Do* in one cycle of change. One should not bundle multiple changes together in one improvement cycle. Rather, they should be prioritized and tested on sequential improvement cycles. Multiple changes will complicate the interpretation of the results and create uncertainty about what change contributed the most to the improvement.

Do

This phase should last only for a defined period of time. It could be minutes, hours, or days, but rarely should it be longer than 2–3 weeks. Remember, these are small tests of change. As in the planning phase, it is important to do only what you can measure and not add other changes in midcycle. In the order entry test above, physicians measured the time it took them to complete the ordering electronically. From the first day, the results were compared to the time it took them to order on paper. In addition, some physicians were directly observed to identify problems in the process.

Study

It is during this phase that the results are reviewed and conclusions made about the relative success of the test. For the order entry example, a few physicians were able to complete the order entry in a shorter time than it took to do paper ordering. Most of the physicians took a longer period of time. They also experienced a good deal of frustration. For instance, if the sequence of steps to do the order entry was not perfect, the user would be thrown out of the process and have to start over at the beginning. It was clear that it wasn't a matter of adaptation, and the change was judged to be a failure after two days.

Act

It is during this phase that one of three things happens. The team should gather, review the data, and make a decision to:

- Determine the change a success and maintain the change to the process
- Determine that the change was a partial success but needs modification
- Determine that the change was a failure and abandon it

In the case of the order entry, the process was abandoned after two days and a new test of change identified. The changes over time included creating a single double-sided form covering all the ordering. Eventually, clerical staff actually completed the detailed work to get the orders implemented. There was some resistance to the change from radiology. The physicians grew tired of trying to negotiate and gave up. It was at this point that I stepped in to get agreement on the new process and form. This is a role that I refer to later in the book when physician leadership is reviewed. It took about two months to complete all the tests of change and get the new process in place. In the end, the physicians were very satisfied with the new process.

Kaizen

Kaizen is a Japanese term that means to "take apart" and "make good." Many people use the term as a substitute for continuous improvement. Kaizen is also used to mean a variety of things in the Lean lexicon; however, for this book, kaizen is meant to refer to a time-limited event focused on a particular process or problem. Kaizen is designed to develop a new process or solution to a problem for which implementation can start immediately at the conclusion of the event. Kaizen events are typically held for more complex problem solving that requires greater time commitment and a cross-functional team. A team will typically consist of a facilitator, frontline staff from the various impacted areas, and supervisors. The decision on whether or not to include supervisors and managers should be made with care, depending on the likelihood of suppressing candid conversation. There are no specific guidelines about the amount of time required in relation to the size of the project. Here are some examples of both continuous improvement projects handled in the course of day-to-day work and kaizen events.

Continuous improvement: Standardizing exam rooms, 6S layouts at nursing stations, single piece flow in medical records, and implementation of a standard simple clinical protocol such as sore throat management.

***Kaizen* events:** Improving changeover times in the operating room, changing rounding patterns for hospitalists to a single unit, establishing fast track in an ED, supply chain management, and a protocol for glucose management throughout the hospital.

Because *kaizen* events are resource intensive, prior planning is a must. In most cases, an organizational champion (leader) should be identified and have the authority to approve the project and the proposed changes. A charter should be created that defines, among other things, the problem, purpose, data, team members, timeline, and costs. A value stream map or process map (depending on the complexity) may need to be developed prior to the beginning of the event.

Events typically last from 1 to 5 days. They contain some distinct phases:

1. Process analysis and observation
2. Identifying opportunities for improvement
3. Testing improvement opportunities by using the improvement model
4. Determining best solutions and developing a management plan to implement, sustain and, if appropriate, spread
5. Presenting final recommendations to champion and other leaders, as needed for approval prior to implementation (typically the last day of the event)

It is vitally important that informal thought leaders from the front lines who are affected participate in the process. Without their participation, the likelihood of sustaining the changes diminishes.

This chapter is a bare bones depiction of a Lean effort. There are many other excellent books that deal with the topic in much more detail.[4,5,6,7] While the focus of this book is on sustaining Lean through physician engagement, throughout you will find material on the implementation phase. I think the likelihood of sustaining Lean is very low if the implementation phase is poorly executed; therefore, there will be additional sections on implementation because of their importance to a successful, sustained transformation.

References

1. Womack, James P., Daniel T. Jones, and Daniel Roos. *The Machine That Changed the World.* New York: Harper Perennial, 1991.
2. Mann, David. *Creating a Lean Culture.* New York: Productivity Press, 2005.
3. Langley, Gerald J., Kevin M. Nolan, Thomas W. Nolan. *The Improvement Guide,* New York: Jossey-Bass, 1996.
4. Graban, Mark. *Lean Hospitals.* New York: Productivity Press, 2009.
5. Hadfield, Debra, RN MSN, Shelagh Holmes, RN. *The Lean Healthcare Pocket Guide XL.* MCS Media, Chelsea, MI, 2008.
6. Henderson, Bruce A. and Larco, Jorge L. *Lean Transformation.* Richmond: The Oaklea Press, 2003.
7. Liker, Jeffery. *The Toyota Way.* New York: McGraw-Hill, 2004.

Chapter 2

Lean and Physician Culture

The Shengo methodology[1] includes a focus on how individuals actually accomplish their work. With this method, staff and physicians are actually videotaped doing their work, a practice known as Full Work Analysis (FWA). Following the taping session, the person who was videotaped reviews the tape second by second with members of the Lean implementation team. This detailed level of analysis about individual work habits can create excitement for the curious and anxiety or resistance for others. The choice of being videotaped is always voluntary. It is very important to assure people that this is not about finding ways to do away with their job; rather, it is to help identify barriers to work efficiency and to help establish best practices for adoption by others. There should be no interaction between the person doing the videotaping and the subject during the actual taping. Such interaction changes the dynamic of the work and detracts from an understanding of what is actually going on. For those who do participate, it is often a very positive experience. It is common to have people comment that "they had never seen themselves work before and learned a lot by doing so."

As a clinician I was able to enter the relatively hidden world of the exam room to videotape physicians during an entire office visit. I emphasized to patients that I was videotaping the physician and would try to totally exclude them from the video. I must admit to being astonished by the variation in how we individually go about both interacting with a patient and physically carrying out the examination. Even within the confines of a standard exam room, moving back and forth between hand sanitizers, sinks, cabinets, exam tables, countertops, and drawers can increase the time of an office visit by 10%–15%. After participating in the process, it was relatively easy for physicians to come to an agreement on standard exam rooms in both the content and location of items.

The combination of using all the tools ensures a focus on both process improvement and individual work habits (Figure 2.1). Some of the tools in the Lean toolkit are an end unto themselves. Single Piece Flow, Level Loading, *Kanban*, and Standard Work can simply be implemented. Value Stream Mapping (VSM), Product Process Flow (PPF), and Full Work Analysis (FWA) are all designed to create improvement ideas and subsequent PDSA cycles or *Kaizen* events. Figure 2.2 shows the relative number of improvement ideas that is typically generated with each tool. By a large margin, PPF and FWA usually generate the greatest number of ideas. This makes sense because VSM is a high-level system type map, and PPF and FWA are very detail oriented.

All Lean implementations are designed to drive out waste. There are eight categories of waste (see Chapter 1). In order to see the waste, most individuals require some training. Most of this

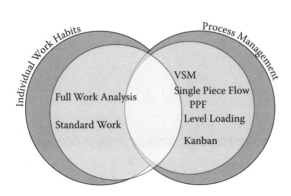

Figure 2.1   Zen diagram of Lean approaches.

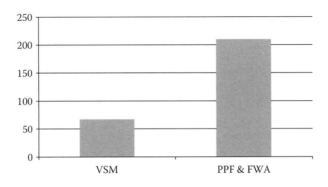

Figure 2.2   Relative number of improvement ideas from VSM, PPF, and FWA.

waste is embedded in small time increments (seconds) in how individuals do their work. Taiichi Ohno (one of the Toyota founders) used to have new managers stand in an eight-foot circle drawn in chalk on the automobile production floor. They were required to report on what they saw. They had to stay in the circle until Mr. Ohno was satisfied that they were seeing all the waste present on the production line. The process is called "Learning to See."

Most physicians monitor and adjust the patient care process on an ongoing basis. For instance, one only has to envision a physician standing at the counter of a nurse's station while documenting a patient chart, reviewing test results, or waiting for someone to retrieve information to understand the opportunity to eliminate waste that many physicians have experienced thousands of times. Physicians stand in Ohno's circle day after day.

This experience frequently leads to complaints about inefficiencies in caring for patients. Rather than embracing the complaints as an opportunity for improvement, they are sometimes viewed as self-serving on the physician's part (the physician's time is more important than the time of others caring for the patient). Alternatively, it can be viewed as just another in a long list of problems administrators are trying to deal with that may never be solved. In some cases, the people responsible simply don't know how to solve the problem. Worse yet, a partial fix is invented to mitigate the problem (see the PICU example in Chapter 1).

If we can be positive about delivering the message about a process problem and identified waste, it can begin to diminish the nonresponsiveness of others. A consistent message about a way to resolve the problem should encourage better responses. Indeed, at Toyota, identification of problems is celebrated as an opportunity to learn and improve. Including a suggestion that using Lean methodologies might resolve the problem permanently provides the administration with a way to approach the problem.

Lean implementations in the healthcare setting, however, pose some unique challenges. Unlike many other quality improvement initiatives, it is virtually impossible to create a Lean environment without impacting or changing various physician work habits. Effective physician leadership is critical for any improvement work involving Lean tools such as Value Stream Mapping and Full Work Analysis. Selection of, and support for, physician leaders as well as engaging frontline physicians in this requires a thoughtful plan. The following problem statement is offered as a background for developing a plan.

Problem Statement: Implementation of Lean Systems Thinking challenges traditional physician autonomy in defining the patient care process.

- Today, some physician's patient care processes are antithetical to Lean principles. Batching routine tasks to the end of the day or hoarding paper medical records pending dictations, lab results, or consultations all create a significant amount of waste for both staff and patients. Lack of standard exam rooms, individual preferences in patient preparation as well as follow-up care will all need to be addressed in order to create a Lean working environment.

- Lean Systems Thinking emphasizes shared work ("moving to the work") when necessary to meet the needs of all the patients of a particular practice. This principle is a cornerstone in primary care when attempting to create a "medical home." Those physicians who have difficulty trusting the work of others will be challenged when faced with a work environment that is absolutely dependent on members of a team working together in a standardized way to care for patients.

- Some physicians may be less willing to provide care for patients whose primary provider is absent. Patients may be more likely sent to urgent care or emergency departments for their acute care needs, subsequently creating unnecessary follow-up appointments with the patient's personal physician. This also leads to a good deal of variation in the patient care experience.

- While not all variations in the individual physician patient care process are critical, some have the potential to disrupt clinical and clerical staff standard work as well as pose patient safety and clinical outcome issues. When other clinicians and clerical staff are working under the principle of "single piece flow" (see the glossary) and a physician is batching tasks, there are bound to be missed messages or lost test results. At the very least, the physician who batches work becomes a constraint against an efficient process.

- Physicians will not always willingly make changes in their work habits. Clinics need a standard approach to working with providers who choose not to change. Most medical staff bylaws, policies, and procedures require action only at fairly destructive levels of dysfunctional behaviors. In a Lean environment, intervention is needed at a much lower threshold. If other staff are required to work in a Lean manner and physicians are allowed to do as they please, the staff is sure to become discontented. The same holds true if individual physicians in a group are allowed to opt out of the standard work created for them.

Initial reactions to the idea of starting Lean will vary from initial enthusiasm to outright resistance. A well-thought-out plan for selecting physician leaders, approaching and engaging others, and dealing with resistance will be required.

Clinical Decision Making and the PDSA Cycle

Clinical decision making has some remarkable similarities to the Plan, Do, Study, Act (PDSA) cycle used for continuous improvement activities both during and after a Lean implementation (see Figure 2.3).

The signs and symptoms that patients present with to the physician are uncommonly immediately diagnostic of the underlying problem that is causing the patients' distress. Therefore, a physician begins a series of steps to determine the root cause and initiate the clinical decision-making process. The steps to accomplish this are also very similar to the PDSA cycle (see Table 2.1).

There are, however, important differences pertaining to expected outcomes and the risk of failure. In the case of a patient with an illness or suffering trauma, the risk of failure from a planned treatment is a worsening clinical condition or, in the worst case, death. From the beginning of their training, physicians are indoctrinated with the importance of choosing the correct treatment plan for ill patients. Incorrect treatment plans can lead to severe consequences, including financial penalties from malpractice awards and loss of livelihood from licensure, credentialing, and privileging sanctions. Experimenting (testing) with a treatment plan is rigorously confined to the scientific method in tightly controlled investigations. Physicians are held to proven standards of care, and any deviation from those standards should be supported by documented variations in the patient condition and circumstances. In continuous improvement work, failure is embraced and incorporated into the learning cycle. The risk from failure is inconsequential when small tests of change are tested in a PDSA cycle.

When a patient has an illness, the goal of the physician plan is to return the patient to health. It is a return to wellness, the steady state that almost everyone wants to be in throughout their lives. Once improvement is achieved, the physician–patient interaction usually decreases. Patients who return to a full state of health typically only see their primary physician at recommended intervals for prevention visits (analogous to assessments done to monitor the health of a process). For patients with a chronic disease, these checkups (assessments) may be scheduled more frequently; however, in the interval between visits, the patient is left to his or her own devices to maintain an improved state of health. In fact, particularly for specialty physicians, in some cases it is not necessary to see the patient again once the patient is restored to health or a prior stable condition.

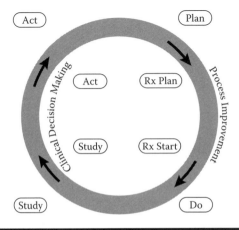

Figure 2.3 Clinical decision making and process improvement (PDSA).

Table 2.1 PDSA and Clinical Decision-Making Steps

Steps in the Clinical Decision-Making Process	Steps in the PDSA Cycle

Plan
 	
• Data gathering
  − Chief complaint
  − History of present illness
  − Social history
  − Family history
  − Physical exam
• Determine diagnosis
	Plan
	
	• Data gathering
	  − Cycle times
	  − Error frequency
	  − Process maps
	  − Staff input
	  − Observe process
	• Determine root cause

Do • Recommend treatment • Patient implements treatment	**Do** • Choose improvement strategy • Team implements strategy
Study • Review results • Re-examine patient	**Study** • Review results • Observe process
Act • Continue treatment • Modify treatment • Stop treatment	**Act** • Keep the change made • Modify the change • Discard the change

In continuous improvement work, the goal is to improve a process, not to return to a prior state or even maintain the current state. Unlike the patient who may not be seen again, the process will be there every day. Unlike a patient, the process (referring to work processes) is there every day and causing dismay (in the case of a poorly functioning process) or delight (from an improved process). If an improved process is not monitored and attempts are made to create even further improvement, it will deteriorate over time. Hence, the term *continuous* improvement is used.

Whether it is primary, secondary, or tertiary prevention, circumstances change. Much like process improvement, the focus is on moving the patient to an improved state of well-being. Except for the absolutely healthiest individuals, the status quo is not acceptable (like many of the processes we deal with on a day-to-day basis in our hospitals and clinics). Because productivity is still the most important driver for healthcare delivery, we are faced with steady pressure to see more patients with less time left for each one. As a consequence, physicians often default to their obligation to be right and simply tell patients what they need to do rather than work with a patient and family to improve the process of how they try to manage their health.

In recent years, the concept of the "planned visit" has been promoted by Ed Wagner, MD, and others as part of developing the "Chronic Care Model." The approach has been shown to be very effective in improving the health of patients. It involves a series of mini-experiments (PDSA cycles) developed in consultation with a patient and family to try small steps toward an improved healthy state. In this model, failure is viewed as an opportunity to reach a deeper understanding about the barriers to the patient's "living process" that have kept the patient from achieving the improvements in daily lifestyle recommended by healthcare providers. The model is also implemented with a team of clinicians (comparable to improvement teams that work to continuously improve processes) to participate in the care plan.

For instance, an overweight diabetic patient who is obese may be frustrated and even avoid follow-up visits when repeatedly reminded of the need to eat better and get more exercise when there has been no success in achieving both tasks. In a planned visit, an attempt would be made to determine root causes for the patient's inability to exercise more and eat better. Perhaps contributing causes might include finances, lack of exercise companions, or safe places to exercise, etc. The next step would be to determine possible next small steps that can be taken to improve the situation. The change would be monitored by a member of the healthcare team and adopted, modified, or discarded based on how effective the strategy was in moving the patient along to improved health.

While we continue to operate in a productivity-driven environment, it will be difficult to implement the planned visit model on a large scale. The point in discussing the approach is to demonstrate that, similar to process improvement, applying the Improvement Model and the PDSA cycle to patient care can achieve improved outcomes.

In summary, I think there are three primary reasons for high levels of engagement and involvement by physicians in a Lean transformation:

1. Although generally true, the old adage that physicians are there to see patients can lead to missed opportunities and waste if the physicians are not significantly involved in Lean transformations. They are smart people, and not tapping into their knowledge and skill creates the eighth deadly waste: loss of talent.
2. Physicians intuitively understand and have been extensively trained in the scientific model and clinical decision making. The similarities to the PDSA cycle make them valuable contributors to continuous process improvement.
3. Physicians will arguably gain more from a Lean implementation than other healthcare workers and perhaps even patients. Patients don't seek care every day, but physicians and staff have to work in the healthcare environment most of the time. They have the biggest stake in seeing the improvements associated with a Lean transformation and will make valuable allies in sustaining the results.

Reference

1. Shingo, Shigeo (translated by Dillon, Andrew). *A Study of the Toyota Production System*. New York: Productivity Press, 1989.

Chapter 3

Creating a Physician Engagement Plan

> What drives the physician is no different from what drives the human spirit. It is the heart and the emotions that change what we do more than anything. … guide leaders and systems toward reconnecting physicians to the place that so many have lost. This is our life and we have worked too hard to miss what is standing right in front of us, shrouded by workload, regulation, personal struggles, and the disillusion that somehow medicine should be more than what we have today.[1]

This quote from Stephen Beeson, MD, is indicative of the beliefs expressed by many physicians I've known. Most of us have grown weary and frustrated with existing workloads and inefficient operational processes. A well-thought-out physician engagement plan is one of the first steps in creating a Lean transformation to address the concerns expressed above.

A Bit of History

How did we get to the point of needing to engage physicians? I am not a historian, but from my perspective, I would start with the 1970s and early 1980s, when there was enough money in healthcare to allow hospitals to cater to physicians as customers. The physicians practiced out of small individual or group practices, but were slowly starting to aggregate into larger groups. Those who were high producers could get just about anything they wanted from the hospitals, particularly if they grouped together by specialty in larger practices.

In the 1980s, the money streams started to diminish while HMOs and managed care were evolving. More and more often, physicians and hospitals found themselves directly competing for the same dollars. Hospitals recognized a risk of losing a referral base and began building tighter relationships with physician groups through an integration in which the hospital, health plan, and medical group agreed to band together to work on the shrinking revenue stream. It was becoming more and more difficult to manage practices effectively. They had to deal with multiple insurance entities. When hospital systems, even those with no ambulatory practice experience, said, "Doctor, you need to practice medicine, and we will run your practices for you," many of us embraced what too frequently turned out to be a hollow promise. Make no mistake about it: we wanted to believe it as much as the hospitals.

Initially, the "opportunity costs" of losing hundreds of thousands of dollars per physician was acceptable to these integrated systems. But as revenue continued to decline, it became less and less tolerable. Physicians were viewed as loss leaders. By the late 1980s and early 1990s, most systems had not been able to figure out how to overcome these losses. Many began to disintegrate and separate from physician groups. In the meantime, revenue streams continued to decrease, and regulatory requirements were increasing.

In many cases, the tension between physician groups and hospital systems continued to grow; however, in a few instances some of the remaining integrated systems or staff model systems began to achieve better financial performance as well as increased quality outcomes. Institutions such as Group Health, Virginia Mason, Thedacare, Mayo Clinic, Denver Health, Geisinger, and other systems in Pittsburgh and Wisconsin gained national prominence (some more recently than others). As I attend national forums, I see some things that most of these organizations have in common. They have physician leadership or strong senior-physician–senior-administrator relationships, they show a strong commitment to quality (many have been pioneers in the work of the Institute for Healthcare Improvement) and, more recently, most have implemented some aspects of Lean consistently over several years.

Have we come full circle to re-engaging physicians by "running the practice for them"? I don't think so. If we are to be successful, it will have to be a meaningful partnership. But I will say that I suspect that while we have been focusing on contracts, competition, regulation, and conflicting goals, inefficiency in offices and hospitals has been a much larger barrier than previously understood. If we are to get through the ever-tightening revenue difficulties, we will have to do it together, and physicians will need to be engaged in that process.

The most important thing about a physician engagement plan is to have one. To enter into a Lean transformation effort without a well-thought-out plan leaves an organization vulnerable to an unsuccessful long-term endeavor. An organization's existing physician engagement plan may lack the specificity needed for a Lean effort. Consequently, whether one already exists or needs to be created, a process that involves current physician leadership should be used to update an old plan or create a new one. I don't want to detract from the need to engage everyone in the organization for a Lean effort to be successful; however, this book will focus exclusively on physician engagement.

Elements of a Physician Engagement Plan

This chapter is not meant to be a complete review of processes to engage physicians. Other works are available with comprehensive approaches.[1,2,3] Rather, the focus will be on aspects of an engagement plan that are very important in a Lean transformation effort. The elements include:

- Creation and communication of vision and goals
- Selection and development of physician champions
- Reward and recognition system
- Approach to and engagement with frontline physicians (Chapter 4)
- Setting expectations for behavior in a Lean culture (Chapter 5)
- The physicians' role in sustaining improvements and maintaining the Lean culture

Vision and Goals

Like all good engagement plans, a compelling vision and clear goals are a cornerstone for beginning the process. A vision/goals statement that contains language such as "create an efficient and error-free work environment" in any relevant clinical area is sure to get a physician's attention. They need to be able to primarily devote their intellectual, emotional, and physical energy to their patients. Inefficient and error-prone work environments are energy drainers that detract from the physicians' ability to care for their patients as well as the patient's subsequent state of health. The 30-second elevator speech might sound something like this:

> Dr. X, you've verbalized your concerns about how difficult it is to get your work done in the hospital. We've decided to do something about it. We are thinking about bringing an approach called Lean Systems Thinking to *improve efficiency and get rid of waste.* It should also allow you to be *more productive.* We would like to have your input and involvement and will be in touch soon.

Of course, the elevator speech by itself will not be adequate to engage the physicians. The news about Lean will need to be routinely and repetitively discussed in newsletters, e-communications, medical staff and department meetings, and committee meetings as well as casual conversations in the hallways and doctors' lounges.

Examples of feasible outcomes that might be incorporated in a vision and goals statement include:

- *Improved workplace efficiency* by as much as 50% reduction in cycle times for labs, pharmacy, OR turnaround, and even meal production for hospitalized patients
- *Improved morale for staff and physicians* by providing clear expectations about work standards
- *Improved* patient satisfaction
- *Increased productivity* by as much as 20% through better flow of patients through clinics, hospitals, EDs, and ORs
- *Decreased cost* by removing unnecessary work and simplifying necessary work processes
- *Improved quality and safety* through the creation of better, more reliable processes

Cost reduction is a sensitive topic and must be dealt with in a forthright fashion. People know that "cost reduction" is sometimes code for staff reduction. One of the common outcomes of a Lean implementation is a reduction in the number of people who are needed to keep a given process working well. In the current healthcare financing environment, many organizations are downsizing on a frequent basis in order to meet budgetary limitations. A common refrain during cost reduction periods that lead to layoffs is the question: "How are we going to get work done now? It was tough enough with the number of employees we had before the layoffs." If an organization is facing layoffs, Lean, rather than being viewed as causing the layoffs, can be viewed as a tool to help us understand how to do the same work more efficiently with fewer people. It can truly result in fulfilling the old adage of "doing more with less."

But people in healthcare are not fools. Everyone knows that cost cutting is associated with potential layoffs, and many are already worried about losing their jobs. Employees are the biggest cost category in healthcare. Regardless of whether an organization is already dealing with downsizing, the issue of cost cutting and joblessness must be dealt with openly. As the result of a recent hospital food services Lean implementation, delivery time of food to patients was reduced from 2 hours to 20 minutes. Patient meals were still hot when delivered. It also resulted in needing 50% fewer employees to prepare and deliver the food. It doesn't take many examples like this to create fear in employees about job loss. Redundant jobs must be reduced through attrition or training and transferred to other unfilled positions in the organization. People will not embrace Lean if they believe it will result in losing their jobs.

As part of its vision and goals statement, a healthcare organization statement *must commit to no layoffs.*

In the tough economic climate of 2010, that is a difficult commitment to make and keep. In fact, keeping the commitment may prolong the time before cost savings are achieved. People are less likely to voluntarily leave their jobs. Alternatives to layoffs or workforce reduction include:

- Transfers to other open positions in the organization
- Training staff to take on jobs that require new skills for an opportunity to move into higher-functioning positions

Or my personal favorite

- Assigning individuals to improvement teams to accelerate needed changes

Selection and Development of Physician Champions

Some characteristics of good physician champions include:

- Enthusiasm and passion
- Puts needs of patients first
- Well respected by staff and peers
- High patient satisfaction
- Some degree of active practice is still part of their work lives
- Previous interest in leadership positions
- Ability to stand firm, if appropriate, when challenged
- Good communication skills

In addition to those generic characteristics, during a Lean transformation, other traits take on more importance as determinants of success. Physician champions for Lean should have demonstrated a long-standing desire to learn. Of course, in healthcare we all have to be learners because the science is changing so rapidly. So, how does "demonstrated long-standing desire to learn" manifest itself? It might be as simple as someone who is curious about most things and asks questions to clarify and show a desire to achieve greater understanding. It could be a willingness to try new things. Typically, dedicated learners are those who would be among the "early adopters" or even innovators in the "Diffusions of Innovation" taxonomy.[4] They would not be among the late adopters and so-called historians, who always use the past to judge success. Lean is about continuous improvement and disciplined experimentation.

A physician champion should not have any conflict aversion tendencies. Lean requires intervention much earlier than is called for in typical hospital bylaws, policies, and procedures. Left unattended, physician behaviors that are not necessarily disruptive but exempt the physician from consensus-based norms will be noticed by peers and staff (see Chapter 6). A champion should not only be comfortable dealing with conflict but also have some skill in bringing recalcitrant physicians into the mainstream of the process. I've found motivational interviewing,[5] a process often used when talking with patients,[6] to be a very useful tool when dealing with physicians who are reluctant to participate in the needed changes.

During one clinic implementation, a frontline physician instructed the medical assistant (MA) to pay no attention and to not participate in what the Lean team was doing. In addition, the physician indicated that the team would be gone later on, and they (the physician and MA) could go back to doing things her way. This put the assistant in the difficult position of potentially being an obstructionist to a successful implementation. My conversation with the physician explored her concerns and what was most important to her about how she performed her work. I made a commitment that nothing would be changed without her input and that every change would be monitored and evaluated for effectiveness. We then negotiated the degree of participation and willingness to try new things she would be willing to accept. Before long, she became an ardent supporter of Lean. It is possible the same outcome would have been achieved if I had simply ignored the issue; however, I think it set an example to her and potentially others about the seriousness of the effort and the transparency required to be successful.

Support and development of physician champions for a Lean effort is a critical factor for successful initiatives. If one physician is selected as an organizational champion for Lean, that person will need to be able to devote substantial time to the role. The champion will need a minimum of 50%, preferably 75%, of his or her time available to "Go to the gemba." The physician champion will need to meet with frontline physicians and staff frequently and repeatedly during the implementation phase and well into the permanent sustainment phase.

The physician champions will need to be well versed in Lean. Typically, they should participate in at least a 5-day course provided either by a consultant group or through other organizations such as the Lean Enterprise Institute (LEI) or the American Society for Quality (ASQ). In addition, these physicians should participate in one or two Lean implementations by being an active member of the team doing the implementation. They should also be knowledgeable about other quality tools and methodologies, particularly the improvement model.[7]

He or she will need to either be well versed in change management or have the resources or partnership of an individual who does. During Lean implementation, it is very important to use change management tools such as stakeholder analysis and be able to identify different forms of resistance from individuals and develop a plan to mitigate the resistance.

A Black Belt colleague shared an experience about a hospitalist team that had a group of four leaders. Early on, the Black Belt had virtually no help from physician leadership to overcome resistance. After multiple meetings where all kinds of problems were posited as barriers to beginning a Lean implementation, progress if any, was minimal. The Black Belt then surveyed other hospitalists, nurses, clerical staff, and others on the units where the Lean effort was to begin. The survey asked people to rate themselves and others relative to resistance to change and to Lean.

It turned out that the four leaders were the most resistant of anyone on the units. Coincident with the survey, senior physician leaders became more involved. They provided a firm but gentle message that Lean was going forward. They worked along with the Black Belt to break down barriers. When the data were shared with hospitalist leaders, they realized that others were enthusiastic about Lean and systematically began to remove the barriers they posited. Currently, the constraint from the old hospitalist model is gone, and other constraints are being identified and eliminated over time.

For the first time, they recently showed a significant reduction in hospital length of stay. The hospitalist team covered two units. Subsequent to the change in attitude and use of Lean tools and new work processes, they were able to reduce the average length of stay (AOLS) from 5.95 to 4.85 days on Unit 1 and 5.27 to 4.77 days on Unit 2. The net revenue effect (assuming all beds continued to be filled) was in excess of $2 million through increased throughput and the consequent increase in the number of patients treated.

Once again, this book is not meant to be a tutorial about change management. There are many companies and consulting firms that offer training in change management, such as the GE Change Acceleration Process (CAP).[8]

Reward and Recognition Plan

The importance of recognizing preferable physician behaviors cannot be overemphasized. One of the best ways to motivate repetition of desired behaviors is through personal recognition.[9] A well-designed program that is reliably implemented will be a powerful force for sustaining initial gains made with Lean. One must be mindful of not providing false or meaningless praise just for the sake of recognition; however, it is unlikely that staff or physicians will become tired of meaningful, well-thought-out recognition. I am not aware of any reported cases of overdose of genuine praise. So, be generous and give freely of praise to both staff and physicians when they've done something to further the advancement of the Lean initiative.

Reward and recognition plans should contain a variety of methods that can be used in different circumstances and settings. I believe financial rewards should come only secondarily through traditional means of increased productivity and incentives for improved quality outcomes. There are, however, other very meaningful ways to not only reward and recognize achievement but also to incentivize physicians to do more and become new leaders for the Lean effort.

While physicians may be singled out for leading particular initiatives, the recognition should not be given in the absence of the team they worked with to achieve their results. Every attempt should be made to have other members of a team present when there are recognition events. Senior leaders and other physician leaders should be vigilant about identifying physicians for potential recognition. One should pay particular attention to those physicians who may have been skeptics in the beginning but have converted to believing in the process and supporting further Lean work.

Internal organizational recognition can be in the form of presentations by the physicians and their teams about their results to senior leaders, boards, peer groups, and at general staff meetings. Recognition opportunities might become a regular part of the agenda for boards, senior leaders, and department meetings. Thedacare has a weekly meeting in which the auditorium is packed with people eager to hear individual improvement teams share the results of their work. It is a powerful way to help spread the innovations to other parts of the organization. Other forms of recognition include newsletter articles, e-mail distributions from senior leaders recognizing the work, as well as good, old word-of-mouth communications.

It is also an excellent idea to include physicians in local or even national media events. We had physicians and staff interviewed by local television stations about the remarkable improvements they achieved. The station was so impressed they aired the piece on a morning show rather than the news, which allowed them more time to devote to the topic.

Approach to and Engagement with Frontline Physicians (Chapter 4)

Before a local implementation begins, several actions should take place to initiate the engagement process. Among these are meetings with physicians and staff to:

■ Determine current site culture, values, and beliefs.
■ Demystify Lean.

- Perform stakeholder analysis.
- Preview what will happen during a Lean implementation.
- Clarify roles physicians may take in the process.
- Set behavioral expectations.

Details about these steps are included in Chapters 4 and 5.

The Physicians' Role in Sustaining Improvements and Maintaining the Lean Culture

David Mann (author of *Creating a Lean Culture*) indicates that

> … Lean can fail immediately, right after the project team moves on, or it can linger until senior leader attention drifts to the next big thing, as far out as 18–24 months. Sustained Lean gains require sustained senior attention, a rare commodity in a quarter-to-quarter environment …. So, in the interim, before new leaders who grew up thinking Lean come into positions of authority, senior management really needs to be diligent about support, teaching and reinforcing Lean practices and behaviors.[10]

The critical time to prevent regression of new work habits into old habits begins immediately after a consultant or implementation team leaves a site. Our teams developed a practice of leaving behind one team member at a site for 2–3 months to help in the early period of sustaining. In the first clinic in which I was involved with an implementation, we decided that we could wait two weeks before placing the sustaining coordinator (Lean specialist) back in the clinic. In the interim, there had been essentially no attention from senior management (or myself, as I was preparing for the next implementation). In just these two weeks, several Lean practices had been abandoned, and people were reverting to old batch processes with which they were familiar with and comfortable at performing. The regression can and does begin immediately in the absence of proper attention from physician champions and senior leaders.

From that point on and going forward for a minimum of two years, local sites will require the support and encouragement of physician champions in addition to other senior leaders. This is the time when most Lean efforts (and other improvement efforts) are most likely to fail. People tend to revert to old work habits and cultures when difficulties are encountered. They will need a physician champion who will be supportive and encouraging, while insisting on keeping the new culture and approach to work intact.

Depending on the size of the organization, there may need to be tiers of physician champions at different levels. Every stand-alone site (clinic, ambulatory surgery, hospital, etc.) should have a physician champion who can dedicate some time to the Lean effort. It may be an existing medical director, but the work should not be added to the person's current duties without additional allocation of time. For small clinics (less than 10 physicians), I would recommend 2–3 hours per week. For larger clinics, a range from a half-day to a full day per week will be needed. Hospital medical staff departments (e.g., medicine, surgery, pediatrics, etc.) will need a physician champion available for the equivalent of one day a week.

Ultimately, every physician will have responsibility for leading and monitoring the Lean approach on a daily basis. Similar to the ED physician (Chapter 1: Standard Work), the frontline physician is in a unique position to observe and intervene when there is lack of adherence to standard work or when Lean tools and methods are abandoned.

This is a big investment because of the need to pay the physicians and, in many cases, provide substantial training; however, the return in cost savings and productivity should far outweigh any concerns about the cost of investment. These physicians will need to be compensated fairly for their time in supporting these programs; however, there needs to be equal emphasis on development and training.

References

1. Stephen C. Beeson, MD. *Engaging Physicians: A Manual to Physician Partnerships*. Gulf Breeze: Fire Starter Publishing, 2009.
2. Jack Silversin and Mary J. Kornacki. *Leading Physicians through Change: How to Achieve and Sustain Results*. Tampa: American College of Physician Executives, 2000.
3. C. Marlena Fiol, Ph.D. and Edward J. O'Connor, Ph.D. *Separately Together: A New Path to Health Hospital Physician Relations*. Chicago: Health Administration Press, 2009.
4. Everett M. Rogers. *Diffusion of Innovations,* 4th edition. New York: The Free Press, 1995.
5. William R. Miller, Ph.D. and Stephen Rollnick, Ph.D. *Motivational Interviewing,* 2nd edition, *Preparing People for Change.* New York. The Guilford Press, 2002.
6. Stephen Rollnick, Ph.D., William R. Miller, Ph.D., and Christopher C. Butler. *Motivational Interviewing in Healthcare.* New York. The Guilford Press, 2008.
7. Gerald I. Langley, Kevin M. Nolan, and Thomas W. Nolan. *The Improvement Guide.* San Francisco: The Jossey-Bass, 1996.
8. George Eckes. *Making Six Sigma Last.* New York: John Wiley & Sons, 2001.
9. Mike Byam. *The WOW! Workplace.* Grand Rapids: The Terryberry Company, 2008.
10. David Mann. Personal e-mail communication. May 6, 2010.

Chapter 4

The Senior Leader's Role

Leadership is the art of getting someone else to do something you want done because he wants to do it.

—Dwight D. Eisenhower

Lean Systems Thinking has been transforming healthcare organizations for several years, resulting in improved quality, lower costs, greater access, higher satisfaction, and a stronger competitive position; however, there have also been several failed deployments where results did not meet expectations. Fortunately, most failures can be avoided by addressing the most common root cause: inactive leadership.

Because Lean represents a systematic, focused approach and a set of tools, it has been used effectively by organizations to address urgent issues; however, the greatest benefit occurs with the realization that successful deployment is about sustained cultural transformation, not about urgent problems, projects, or tools. Transformation is about breakthrough improvement, not incremental improvement.

Success Starts at the Top

Achieving a successful transformation is impossible without the leaders of the organization being active supporters. Leaders set the stage and the context. Without senior leadership's active and enthusiastic involvement, benefits will be limited to, at best, sporadic successes in individual departments rather than organizational transformation.

> We were frustrated because the transformation seemed to be stalling or rolling backward in some areas.........We were demanding change of everyone while we the senior leadership, remained unchanged.....We were hierarchical and autocratic, keeping a tight grip on all the cards.[1]

Leadership Is More Important Than Tools

There is a popular aphorism in business that states "Culture Eats Strategy for Lunch." While this is obviously not meant to be taken literally, it does emphasize that organizational change and transformation must be aligned with culture—and it is senior leadership, along with physician leaders, that establishes and reinforces the culture.

Major transformation will not occur easily for many reasons. Inertia and complacency are rampant, and strong leadership is needed to overcome those powerful organizational forces. Also, employees feel comfortable doing things the way they have been done for years, and change is often threatening.

The Senior Leader's Role

Creating an effective cultural transformation requires many duties and continual effort. To be effective, the senior leader must establish a process that includes the following steps for leading the transformation.

Important Duties of a Leader

- Create the vision.
- Select the right people.
- Create and oversee the Deployment Plan.
- Provide adequate resources.
- Train and educate.
- Invest in infrastructure.
- Establish metrics for success.
- Select projects that align with organizational priorities.
- Communicate frequently and passionately.
- Create a process for monitoring progress.
- Sustain and spread gains.

Create the Vision—Determine the Right Destination before You Start the Journey

A common reason why the process improvement journey fails in many organizations is that there is no clear agreement on the vision or just what the right destination is. Specifically, they make no connection between aligning the business needs of the organization—the true purpose of any process improvement—with the deployment of the Lean effort.

People in the organization will want to know where the transformation is headed, what the destination is, and what success will look like when there is progress. Often, it is not possible to describe a *final* destination, so interim goals are helpful and serve as stepping stones to success. Once an interim destination is reached, it's time to pick another destination, farther along the path toward perfection, that materially benefits the organization.

The visions I have found to be most effective can be communicated in a minute or less. They are clear and inspiring—and describe how the customer will benefit, not just how the organization will prosper.

Selecting the Right People

An important role for senior leaders is recruitment, selection, training, and retention of a talented team to fill key Lean/quality improvement roles. These roles are not for the timid—this team will be leading important projects that effectively transform current operations. They are change agents.

Selection of team members is critical to a successful deployment of a Lean transformation effort. It is the responsibility of senior leaders to establish a process for selecting a talented and motivated team. While using the correct Lean tools in the correct situation is important, it is the people deploying and using the tools who determine the level of success.

A blend of strong technical capability and effective change management skills is needed.

Individuals should be more than just self-trained and certified as either Lean specialists, Lean Six Sigma Black Belts (LSSBB), or Master Black Belts. Individuals should also have several years of experience. While not absolutely required, experience in healthcare is highly desirable. The start-up will be difficult for someone with no experience in healthcare because of the need to assimilate a new language, technical knowledge, culture, and beliefs.

Provide Resources and Invest in Infrastructure

Successful deployment, similar to any worthy endeavor, requires an investment—primarily in human resources—to adequately support the effort.

The primary investment revolves around key roles:

- Deployment team—Lean specialists, LSSBB, Lean specialists in training, and other support staff who receive comprehensive training and are devoted full-time to process improvement, design, and management.
- Project teams—time away from regular duties for those who work in areas that are involved in process improvement projects. This is an area that is often underinvested in and can result in frustration and results that fall short of potential.
- Training—time away from regular duties to attend training on use of tools and process for project deployment. Workshops are most effective when they are *Just-in-Time*, meaning just before when the deployment will occur in the area. If designed and implemented properly, the sessions will not only inform but also inspire people to see the benefits and embrace the concepts of Lean. Senior leaders must also be committed to be trained in Lean principles, tools, and embrace the cultural change needed for a successful transformation.
- Incentive compensation—organizations often devote a percentage of incentive compensation for accomplishment of Lean goals.
- Infrastructure support—from key system areas, such as Finance, Human Resources, IT; they must be willing to change internal policies and procedures to support implementation.

While investments can seem daunting, Lean projects often achieve first-year returns that exceed investment and typically have a very high ROI.

Executive and Champion Role Definition and Training

A comprehensive training program for each of the Lean roles is a key element in successful deployment. The executive leadership team plays a crucial role in the launch of the Lean program. An important step in creating enthusiasm and focus is an initial workshop for senior leaders, who have a critical role to play in the deployment. The purpose of the session is to educate them about the basics of the tools, what they can expect to accomplish, and the special role leaders will play. Invitees should include:

- All vice presidents and members of the senior leadership team, including the CEO
- Key representatives from:
  - Human resources
  - Informatics
  - Finance
- In-house training departments that may have to assume the educational responsibilities in the future

This executive team will establish a process of regularly overseeing and tracking progress and attending periodic reviews to understand project status, assign needed resources, and remove obstacles. A robust process is critical because inactive leadership is typically a root cause of failed deployments. The commitment to the senior leader role must be serious, or there will be adverse consequences.

After senior leaders and champions are educated, business unit managers and staff are also given in-depth training about Lean and the changes that can be expected in their area. Also, as more people are hired by the organization, there will be a need for continuous training on an indefinite basis.

Frequent and Clear Communication

Send clear and frequent messages that Lean and process improvement are a key priority for the organization. One of the first organizations to deploy Six Sigma was GE. Early in their deployment, CEO Jack Welch described a number of quality concerns and issued a brief statement explaining that GE was about to embark on a major initiative to address them. He stated that he felt the initiative would be the most important priority for the organization for the next five years and that GE would be a very different company as a result of it. He provided a "burning platform," created a sense of urgency, and maintained a clear focus on the effort.

An effective method of communication used by the inventors of Lean is *Going to the Gemba*, which is a Japanese term for spending time at the place where the work is actually done. People who work in areas where process improvement projects are deployed become much more engaged and view the deployment as a priority when they see the leaders in their areas.

Strategic Alignment

Deployment of Lean is not an end in itself—it is a means of achieving organizational strategy, vision, and goals. Senior leaders create the long-range strategy and have to align the Lean deployment to it. Commitment and buy-in will be much higher if people in the organization see that deployment is a tool for accomplishing the important strategic goals—not just another thing to do.

Deployment Plan

Overseeing the creation of a deployment plan that identifies the major elements of a successful implementation is an important role of a senior leader. The deployment plan should include, at a minimum, the following elements:

- Executive Champion Role Definition and Clarity
- Physician Engagement Plan

- Communication Plan
- Lean Specialist Recruitment and Selection
- Project Selection and Prioritization
- Training Plan
- Infrastructure Development
- Performance Measures
- Project Reporting, Tracking, and Auditing
- Project Spread
- Sustainability

The deployment is ongoing, and the major "chapters" should include a timeline and identification of the leader responsible for completion. Most organizations have benefited from advisors who have experience in prior successful deployments.

Establish Measures for Success

What an organization measures is what people will focus on. A huge benefit of Lean is that it includes a very robust quantitative emphasis—there is nowhere to hide. It is the leader's role to determine metrics—both outcome and in-process—that allow everyone to know exactly where each project and the overall effort stand at any given time. Outcome measures focus on results, and in-process measures provide real-time information that acts as an early warning system to identify problems before they arise.

People throughout the organization will quickly learn what areas the CEO and others on the executive team feel are important by noticing what measures are being tracked. A Project Reporting and Tracking System, along with a disciplined process for regular reporting, allows managers to know what is being reviewed and when.

Project Spread and Sustainability

Even when there are tremendous gains, it is very easy to slip back to old habits and processes. When the deployment begins to mature, there will be a large number of completed projects that will require continual monitoring so that achievement levels don't drop. When senior leaders actively participate and guide the process, others quickly notice that maintaining the process changes that resulted in gains is important.

Perhaps one of the most important roles for a senior leader during this phase is to maintain the pace of the deployment (spread). All too often, when organizations experience initial success, the desire to accelerate the spread develops. Pressure may mount to shorten implementation cycle times and mandate that successful changes at a site be implemented everywhere without going through the Lean process. I've experienced attempts to do so in different settings, and the results are invariably less than successful and are often harmful. The senior leader must keep the deployment at a prescribed pace. Acceleration should only be attempted by increasing resources to be able to execute more implementations simultaneously.

The senior leader must also maintain a close relationship with the physician leader for the Lean effort. A process to monitor not only new implementations, but more importantly, those sites that are in the sustain phase has to be maintained. The monitoring process should include a methodology that will reveal any degradation in process performance and, as a result, trigger quick and early intervention.

All of this will require a significant reallocation of senior leader time. The oversight responsibility will require a significant amount of time and should not be delegated away to others.

Summary—Active Leadership Is Essential to Effective Deployment

Leadership that is active, involved, and engaged in the deployment—before, during, and ongoing—is the most essential factor in a successful deployment. On the other hand, lack of leadership has been seen as the most common root cause of deployments that have not lived up to expectations.

Reference

1. John Toussaint, Roger A. Gerard, and Emily Adams. *On the Mend: Revolutionizing Health Care to Save Lives and Transform the Industry.* Cambridge: Lean Enterprise Institute, Inc. 2010.

Chapter 5

Analysis and Preparation

Large systems with multiple sites should go through an analysis process to select and prioritize locations for initial implementation efforts. The adage that "success breeds success" is particularly true in larger organizations where there will be multiple site implementations. If early implementations are viewed as failures, subsequent success will become very difficult. There is no right method for selecting initial sites, but there are several factors that should be considered, including business needs, operational impact, and state of readiness. A more detailed analysis and preparation process should follow site selection.

Business Needs Assessment and Operational Impact

There are many locations in healthcare systems where Lean, when applied properly, will have a significant impact on cost, productivity, quality, and satisfaction for patients, employees, and physicians. Prime locations include operating suites, emergency departments, labs, imaging facilities, larger clinics, pharmacies, and hospital wards. There are a great number of variables associated with selecting a unit to begin a Lean process; however, it is possible to make some assumptions about potential success based on the prior experience of others. Each area typically has its own set of strengths and challenges. For instance, emergency departments can produce financial returns for decreasing the number of patients left without being seen, but capital is often required to change layouts. Hospital wards can produce ROI through reduced length of stay and increased throughput, but require a high degree of physician acceptance of changes to rounding.[1] Where to start would depend on an individual institution's needs, wants, and goals as well as the current performance of a given location. Three categories of factors to consider include the following:

- Organizational Lean resources
- Likelihood of financial, quality, or satisfaction improvement
- Site readiness

Lean Resources

It would be wonderful if a healthcare leadership team or CEO were to have an epiphany about Lean as a system-wide strategy for improvement followed by a systemic strategic plan to commit to that journey. Most organizations don't start their Lean journey with a comprehensive strategic design for Lean. That would require a major financial investment and significant commitment of people and other resources. Alternatively, I have seen the physician leaders of a large academic center successfully lobby for a Lean effort at their institution, where senior leadership appears to be attuned to physicians' needs. Consequently, what started out as a project-by-project attempt will change to an organization-wide systemic effort to introduce Lean. Practically speaking, the journey more often begins on a project-by-project basis, with overall organizational commitment coming later in the process. It seems that, more often than not, early smaller successes are needed for broader organizational commitment to follow.

Most organizations do not start a Lean effort with a well-organized full complement of Lean specialists. It is not uncommon for staff from a quality department or elsewhere in the organization to attend training for Lean and even become certified, return home, and begin a Lean project. In my opinion, this is a "surefire recipe for disaster." The likelihood of a successful implementation in this case is very low. It is particularly damaging to future Lean endeavors if the failed project is portrayed as a Lean effort. Lack of success can lead to subsequent rejoinders similar to "we tried Lean and it did not work." Conversely, if initial attempts are successful, it can lead to a false sense of security regarding the organization's capability to achieve a more comprehensive Lean transformation.

More commonly, the staff exposed to Lean success stories become advocates for starting a Lean journey in the organization. These partially trained but inexperienced people, rather than trying to start a Lean project themselves, lobby to obtain organizational resources, either through hiring Master Lean or Lean Six Sigma black belts or obtaining the services of a consultant to lead a project.

In these smaller project-oriented Lean efforts, there are typically one or, at most two, experienced Lean specialists to lead the effort. Consequently, there should be one, at most two, initial projects. At a minimum, the organization needs to commit to an experienced Lean specialist leader capable of teaching others and 4 or 5 of the best and brightest staff from the designated site who will step out of their usual roles for 3 months to participate on the Lean implementation team. Many organizations will struggle to make even this level of commitment in the early stages of the Lean journey. This makes selection of initial sites very important in developing an organizational will to deploy Lean throughout the organization.

Likelihood of Financial, Quality, or Satisfaction Improvements

Organizations may have different priorities for improvement efforts based on their individual circumstances. While better financial performance as well as improved quality and satisfaction are universal goals for all institutions, there may be greater needs in one area or another. In 2010, healthcare financing is the primary focus of most institutions and practices. While improving quality and satisfaction is almost always the product of a Lean implementation, I would not recommend Lean as the primary approach to gaining improvement. I have come to believe that waste in our systems must be removed before being able to demonstrate sustainable quality improvement. Other tools, such as those used in Six Sigma, work to reduce variation and are more focused specifically on quality outcomes. Other evidence-based strategies[2] are preferable for improving patient satisfaction.

Lean is about getting rid of waste and consequent cost and low productivity. For institutions needing to show financial improvement, there are many evidence-based examples of Lean leading to efficiency and improved productivity in all settings referred to earlier.[1]

Larger returns on the investment typically are shown in operating suites, emergency departments, and large ambulatory centers; however, I want to caution again that returns are based on local circumstances. An operating suite with quick turnaround times, good inventory control, and tightly managed, efficient staff will probably not show as much gain from Lean as one with lesser performance metrics. That does not mean that Lean should not be implemented in these circumstances; however, if one is looking to produce dramatic results in early Lean work, it might be better to select a site that is not already functioning at a high level.

Resources

When selecting a site, the resources and performance of the site itself should be evaluated in addition to the overall organizational resources. There are many factors to consider when selecting an early site in a Lean journey. They include:

- Status of administrative and physician leadership for the site
- Desire to improve
- Architecture of the location
- Culture

Leadership

A strong leadership team will be required for a Lean implementation to be successful. There are times during a Lean implementation when leadership skills will be severely tested. When one changes the work culture of a site, there will be ensuing behavioral issues that will need to be addressed by leaders. Locations where there are vacancies in either administrative or physician leadership positions or with autocratic/authoritarian top-down leadership styles may not make ideal candidates for early implementation. Those circumstances would be an indication to wait until the positions are filled or for adoption of a new management style. Mediocre, or worse yet, poorly performing managers and leaders should either be coached or replaced before starting. Conversely, a high-performing manager or leader who is not willing to commit the time and embrace Lean may be more difficult to deal with than filling a vacant position. If staff and other physicians see the leader not committing to the effort, they will believe they don't have to either.

I want to emphasize here that coaching should be attempted for leaders who are not performing as well as their peers. One of the amazing things that occurs during a Lean implementation is that there are instances of both poorly functioning staff and leaders who transform themselves into strong performers. It is a difficult balancing act between risk of failure because of poor leadership and giving everyone a chance to be successful; however, in the early stages of a Lean implementation, one should err on the side of going only to sites with strong leadership, saving those lacking this vital component until a later date after the gap in leadership has been resolved.

In one case, we did move a manager who, after coaching, showed little improvement, to another location and brought in a highly effective manager before starting. The site was eventually one of the most successful in the system. In the meantime, more coaching and mentoring were provided to the displaced manager in anticipation that Lean would eventually come to that manager's location.

Desire to Improve

One might make the argument that a good starting place would be a site that is highly successful. I think one should be particularly careful in this case. A successful site (by whatever means one judges success) may be an appropriate one *if* it is accompanied by a strong desire to improve. In a location where the staff, physicians, and leaders believe they are successful because of how they do their work *and* resist change because of that belief, successful implementation will be more difficult. I call this "pride of ownership." It can be a powerful deterrent to success.

Conversely, there may be poorly functioning sites, known as "brown fields" in Lean lexicon, that may be good candidates for improvement. If the leaders and staff truly want to improve and perhaps have unsuccessfully tried different improvement methodologies in the past, creating a sense of desperation, large improvements can be achieved. Desperation can be a powerful breeder of motivation and innovation, which, in turn, will make for a more successful initiative.

There is no right answer here; however, the one common thread in either situation is a strong desire to improve.

Architecture

As part of the pre-assessment process, a *gemba* walk is a must if for no other reason than to experience the architecture of the location. Traditional architectural layouts in healthcare settings often present barriers to successful Lean operations. The ability to see and to be close to patients and work areas is a key factor. It is, at times, subtle, and only an experienced Lean specialist can identify problems.

I participated in the design of one of my pediatric group's new offices and thought we had an efficient design. The problem was that I had looked only at horizontal blueprints and a limited mock-up. We did not create a floor-to-ceiling mock-up. We only laid out workstations. The design was partially based on an already successful design in our practice. The first day I walked in after sheetrock was on the walls, I realized we were in trouble. There were 4 support columns and walls in the central work area that obstructed 70% of the view. You could talk with someone, then walk away, and within 10 seconds not be able to see them. Consequently, we spent a lot of wasted time looking for each other (see Figure 5.1).

If lines of sight are obstructed or walking long distances to retrieve needed materials is required, the organization must be ready to invest in some remodeling or relocation of work materials. If not, outcomes from Lean may be limited.

Readiness

An assessment of the site's beliefs, values, and culture will be critical prior to implementation. Table 5.1 represents a culture survey tool that can be used along with other tools to determine the baseline state of readiness. It can be used to compare with future results to reflect progress in creating a Lean culture.

Information obtained in the survey should allow one to help build a profile regarding employee empowerment, problem-solving strategies, management styles, and commitment to quality improvement. The survey has not been validated for correlation with actual situations at a site, but can be used to track, on a serial basis, some of the important culture elements for sustaining Lean. Not all of the agree/disagree questions relate to key elements, but some examples include the following.

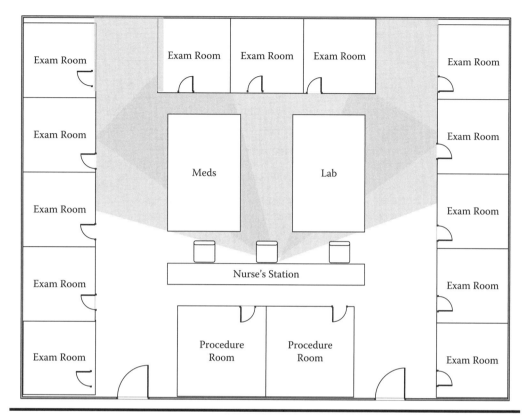

Figure 5.1 Decreased visual fields secondary to design.

Standard Work

- I do not know exactly what is expected of me in my job.
- Everyone in my work area follows the same method for getting similar work done.
- Every person receiving care at this clinic experiences a consistent patient care experience.
- I use "work-arounds" for many of my work processes.
- I have the tools, space, and information I need to do my work well.

Management Style

- Work teams actively problem-solve without needing to involve management.
- I do not receive recognition for good work.
- Management gives me real-time performance feedback.
- Management responds quickly to my needs and suggestions.
- Management discourages me from identifying problems in my work.

Commitment to Quality Improvement

- Quality is a top priority in my work area.
- I know how to measure the quality of my work.

Table 5.1 Lean Culture Survey

Please Place an "X" in the Rating Category that Best Describes your Level of Agreement or Disagreement with Each Statement Below	1	2	3	4	5
I feel free to make suggestions for improvement					
Work teams actively problem-solve without needing to involve management					
Management discourages me from identifying problems in my work					
I feel supported to speak up if I see something that will negatively impact patient care					
I do not know exactly what is expected of me in my job					
Everyone in my work area follows the same method for getting similar work done					
Every person receiving care at this clinic experiences a consistent patient care experience					
I use "work-arounds" for many of my work processes					
Our organization uses metrics effectively to measure improvement					
I know how to measure the quality of my work					
I do not receive recognition for good work					
Management gives me real-time performance feedback					
I have the tools, space, and information I need to do my work well					
We have good processes for doing our work					
I typically do not have everything I need within easy reach to do my job					
The people I work with cooperate and work as a team					
Quality is a top priority in my work area					
Employees in my work area rarely take personal ownership of their work processes					
I have opportunities at work to learn and grow					
Management displays positive and supportive leadership for change					
My manager is not capable of effectively coaching our team through change					
Management responds quickly to my needs and suggestions					
I spend most of my day doing things that are a waste of time					
1 = strongly disagree 2 = disagree 3 = neither agree nor disagree 4 = agree 5 = strongly agree.					

Table 5.2   Interview Survey

PRE-LEAN ASSESSMENT

SITE:_____	DATE _____

Describe three things the site is most proud of and would not want to lose:

Be persistent in eliciting responses to this question. People are often reluctant to respond to positive questions. The answers should be saved and used as a guideline when considering individual improvement activities that might pose a threat to these beliefs.

Describe the priority for Lean in comparison to other goals for the site:

Sites will have different reasons for implementing Lean. Some may be enthusiastic and have either realistic or unrealistic expectations for outcomes. Others may be passive, and may be participating only because it is an organizational mandate. Each situation requires a different response and exploration of underlying beliefs. This is also a good opportunity to understand the overall knowledge level of people who work in the site.

Describe current or planned projects for the site:

It is important to understand how many other projects are going on at the site. While it involves subjective judgment, the presence of more than 1 or 2 minor projects will be a significant obstacle to overcome if Lean is to be successful. If there are more projects, serious consideration should be given to rescheduling the Lean effort to another time with fewer conflicting priorities. There is only so much energy available from the people involved to devote to change efforts.

Describe the current status of leadership for the unit:

- Physician leadership: Is there a void in leadership? If so, consider rescheduling until the void is filled. Have the physician leaders been involved in the decision and are they advocates? If not, a plan should put in place to address the gap.
- Administrative/nursing leadership: Is there a void in leadership? If so, consider rescheduling until the void is filled. Have the administrative leaders been involved in the decision and are they advocates? If not, a plan should put in place to address the gap.

Describe the decision-making process for the site:

Are decisions made in a top-down, authoritarian manner? Is the process consensual? What gaps exist in how physicians and managers make decisions compared to how they will need to in a Lean environment? If there are deficits, a plan should include strategies to work on this.

Describe current beliefs about what improvements are needed/desired for the site:

What is important to people at the site? They may not become the priority focus of actual improvement projects or activities during the Lean implementation; however, it is important to capture the ideas and ensure, if possible, that they are included in the complete Lean improvement project list.

(Continued)

Table 5.2   Interview Survey (Continued)

PRE-LEAN ASSESSMENT
SITE:_____   DATE _____
Describe the outcomes the site would like to achieve through Lean implementation:
This is another question designed to identify both realistic and unrealistic expectations for a Lean effort. Addressing the unrealistic expectations early in the process will help avoid disappointment later.
Describe perceived barriers/obstacles to a successful Lean transformation:
Explore physical layout, attitudes, staffing shortages, etc.
Describe previous improvement efforts and the outcomes:
What were previous attempts at improvement work and what were the outcomes? If they were initially successful, were they sustained?
Describe gemba walk observations:
Do a gemba walk with a few people from the site to answer any questions you may have. Key items to take note of include architectural issues, organization of workstations, the eight deadly wastes, varying intensity of work among individuals (do people appear to be inactive, waiting for something, etc.).

Pre-implementation interviews should also be a part of the assessment. Refer to Table 5.2 for an example of interview questions I have used when assessing a site before implementation. Some of the rationale for the questions and suggestions on how to use them are in italic print following the topic headers. Management leaders and physician leaders should be interviewed. In addition, a representative of different work groups (nursing, medical assistants, clerks, etc.) should be included. In my experience, the interviews would take 30 to 45 minutes, depending on whether they are conducted individually or in groups of 2 or 3. I would not recommend larger groups. It has been my experience that the quality of information is better in small groups.

It is here that an implementation team should pause briefly and review what it has learned. The strengths and weaknesses of a location should be noted and a plan developed to both address weaknesses and leverage strengths. Individuals with a particular affinity for Lean might be identified as team members or leaders. Conversely, if management styles are not conducive to maintaining a Lean culture, a coaching plan should be part of the implementation strategy.

It is also possible that deficiencies could be identified that would indicate that the implementation should be canceled or delayed. In one clinic, the architectural issues were so great that we had to obtain organizational commitment to remodel to open up visual site lines. Had they been unable to make the commitment, the implementation probably would have been delayed into another budget cycle, when remodeling could occur.

The information obtained as discussed above should then be used to complete a plan of implementation. The plan should include the elements contained in a site charter (see below) as well as any plans about special circumstances. Architectural, leadership development, and cultural issues may need to be addressed as separate items in the plan. Because of the sensitive nature of some of the issues, they would not be shared in a public plan such as a charter.

Preparation Phase

Now that the baseline assessment phase is completed, what I call the "preparation phase" should begin through interaction and dialogue with the staff and physicians. It is at this point that the physician (and staff) engagement process begins in earnest (Figure 5.2).

An initial Just In Time (JIT) meeting with staff and physicians should be held to educate, clarify, and explore individuals' hopes and fears about the Lean journey. This meeting should be held about a week before the implementation is scheduled to begin. A minimum of two hours (which can be staggered as multiple sessions in order to include all staff and physicians) should be devoted to this portion.

A typical agenda might include:

1. Introductions: of Lean team members, senior leaders who attend, and site leadership teams.
2. Healthcare environmental reasons for pursuing Lean: include national and local trends as well as organizational history. Discuss why the organization chose Lean over other alternative approaches to improvement.
3. Stakeholder analysis: (see the following description) Based on the assumption that Lean will be successful.

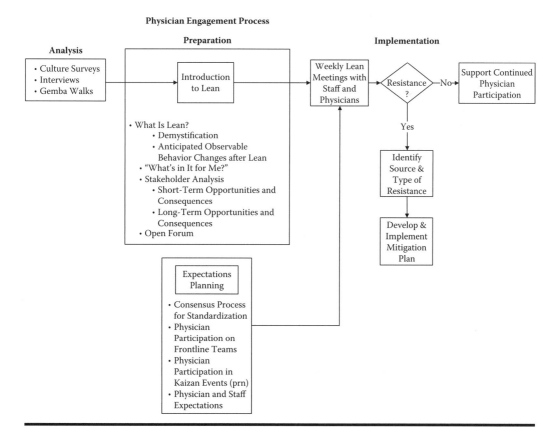

Figure 5.2 Physician engagement process.

4. Education presentation about Lean: to include:
   a. Elements and tools of Lean.
   b. Practical exercises.
   c. Results obtained by others.
   d. What they can expect to happen at their site. Focusing especially on what will happen in the first 2–3 weeks when value stream mapping is occurring will be helpful to the people at the site. Typically, people expect things to change right away. It can be reassuring for them that the initial phase is about detailed analysis of their work. A phrase I often use to explain this initial period is that it is like walking in their shoes "on steroids" for the person analyzing the work patterns.
5. Open a dialogue to answer questions.

Stakeholder Analysis

I've found that just about everyone in healthcare is aware of the changing economic climate and the many challenges facing the industry. By the time you are in the preparation phase, everyone should know that a Lean initiative will be starting in the organization and the rationale for doing so; however, it is a good time to review the factors leading to the decision to do Lean.

As a result, I recommend a modified stakeholder analysis by focusing on a topic. In this case, the topic is creating a successful Lean transformation. It can be used to elicit individual and group fears and hopes about Lean. It also is a good segue into a discussion designed to educate and demystify Lean (Table 5.3).

At this point, the information in the stakeholder analysis will be created based on people's beliefs, which will have been influenced by what they have heard or read about Lean. The purpose here is not to make an informed decision about proceeding; that decision will have already been made. It is really to elicit everyone's anxieties, hopes, fears, and beliefs about Lean.

Site leaders and physicians should begin a parallel process (usually one or two meetings at most) to set expectations for participation, acceptable behavior, and methodologies for reaching consensus about standardization issues.

Physicians will need to make decisions about standard exam and procedure rooms both in terms of content and layout. Forms and work processes, such as patient notification for lab or x-ray

Table 5.3   Modified Stakeholder Analysis

Consequences of Completing a Lean Transformation	
Short-Term Negatives	**Short-Term Positives**
Long-Term Negatives	**Long-Term Positives**
Steps in Stakeholder Analysis (30 minutes)	
1. Gather as many staff and providers as possible.	
2. Brainstorm ideas and record them in the 4-quadrant tool above.	
3. Be prepared to provide ideas and comments on your own to ensure completeness.	
4. Debrief the 4 quadrants and organizational mandates to do the new work.	

LEAN Project Charter		
Resource Plan	*General Information*	*Review Timing*
Project No.:	**Business/ Business Unit:**	**Implementation Start Date**
Lean Team:	**Current Cost of Poor Quality:**	1 Jan 2011
	• Unnecessary office visits	**Implementation End Date**
Champion:	• Long wait times	31 Mar 2011
	• Lost reports leading to patient harm	
Process Owner:		**Toll Gate (Review) Dates**
	• Excess inventory	1 Feb, 1 Mar, 1 Apr
	• Poor patient satisfaction	
	Project Overview	

Problem Statement: Current financial performance at site "x" is exceeding budget, morale is low, and excess errors are occurring

Goal Statement: To reduce cost by 30% in 1 year and increase employee and physician satisfaction by 10% in 6 months

Current Baseline Performance:

• Budget performance

• Satisfaction scores

• Cycle times

• Access delays

• Etc.

Business Case Analysis: Reasons for this site selection

Items In Scope: Patient visit from the time of request for an appointment to completion of the visit
Items Out of Scope: Lab, x-ray

Resources/Team Members and Functional Area:

Signatures

Champion:	Project Team Leader:	

Actual Benefits (savings, metric reduction): To be completed at 6-month intervals after implementation

Figure 5.3 Site implementation charter.

results, will need to be standardized. How will they do that? Will individuals or small teams be given authority or will the group as a whole need to decide?

There will be a need for physicians to have inputs into improvement team decision-making. There may be several teams at any given time. A site should have weekly meetings that are open forums for staff and physicians to receive progress reports and updates as well as ask questions and provide feedback. Daily Lean core team meetings will be occurring that will need periodic physician participation. What will be required from individual physicians? Will they be compensated for their time?

Finally, it must be made clear that in the early stages of a Lean implementation, there may be a good deal of emotional stress. When you start changing how people do their work, emotional stability may become labile, with resultant unwanted behaviors emerging. How will those behaviors be dealt with and by whom? Are there new rules that need to be in place, either temporarily or permanently (see Chapter 6)?

The document should include expectations for both positive and negative behaviors. Expectations for participation on improvement teams and attendance at Lean meetings should be included. Subsequently, site leadership should present the proposal to the staff for acceptance or modification.

A final step is the creation of a site-specific charter. A charter is a cornerstone document that details expectations about timelines, accountabilities, and deliverables. It should be used as a reference point to measure progress in the months after the implementation. It should be signed by the champion (usually a senior leader with reporting responsibility for the area) and the process owner (typically a manager in a clinic, an OR director or manager, etc.). It should be available for review when assessing progress (tollgate meetings). Typical content is included in italics in the charter (see Figure 5.3).

References

1. Charles Protzman, George Mayzell, and Joyce Kerpchar. *Leveraging Lean in Healthcare.* CRC Press: Taylor & Francis, Boca Rafon, 2010.
2. Studer, Quint. *Hardwiring Excellence.* Gulf Breeze: Fire Starter Publishing, 2003.

Chapter 6

Setting Expectations

Setting behavioral standards and expectations may not seem like the best way to engage physicians; however, in the absence of those standards, when a conscientious physician is reluctantly participating in a change and notices others who are just opting out without consequences, negativism is sure to follow. Transparency is a key ingredient in a Lean implementation. Physicians and staff need to participate in agreed-upon ways. One of the tools I've found helpful is to get agreement that, if a physician is unhappy with a change or process, it should be taken to the Lean team rather than just having the physician opt out, or worse, sabotage the efforts of the team. Staff will also notice very quickly if some physicians are allowed to not participate or not adhere to consensus-based standards. Consequently, resentment will build.

Most behavioral expectations are clarified and set at the local level just prior to starting a Lean implementation; however, an acceptable overall organizational framework for those expectations needs to be set prior to meeting with frontline physicians. The organizational effort here is akin to defining the boundaries of the playing field with the definitions of what goes on in the field of play held primarily at the local level. Senior physician leaders as well as frontline physicians recognized as thought leaders should participate on the team creating the organizational expectations.

Setting expectations for behavior during, and for participation in, Lean efforts is a critical element for successful physician engagement. Perhaps it is more accurate to describe a physician engagement plan as a physician *disengagement prevention* plan. As one moves further into a Lean transformation, difficult changes in work habits will be required. Some physicians will embrace the changes, particularly after they recognize improvements in operating efficiency. Others will have difficulty with the changes. There undoubtedly will be those who actively resist the changes. Some will passively try to avoid acceptance and participation. Finally, there will be some who will never be able to adopt the changes and will need to choose a different working environment.

People adopt innovation (Lean should certainly be recognized as an innovation) at different rates. Diffusion of innovation through a population occurs at predictable rates[1] (see Figure 6.1). There is a balance between allowing time for slow adopters and not allowing resentment to build among other physicians and staff for their perceived lack of participation. Maintaining the balance is not always easy.

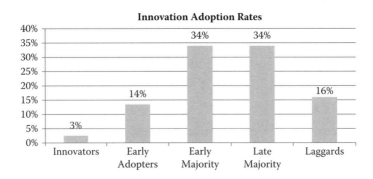

Innovation Adoption Rates

Figure 6.1   Innovation adoption categories. (Adapted from *Diffusion of Innovations*, fourth edition, Everett Rodgers, 1995. The Free Press, New York.)

The pace of adoption can be affected by many factors, but the use of mandates is particularly powerful and tempting; however, using mandates is associated with high costs over time in the form of resentment, early abandonment of new practices, and potentially increased staff turnover. Mandates should be used only as a last resort.

For those physicians who embrace the change, a lack of acceptance by their peers will have minimal, if any, impact on their continued adoption of the new work habits; however, a large number of physicians will be middle-to-late adopters.[1] They may be reluctantly trying the changes required. If peers appear to be able to opt out without consequences, a powerful precedent is set, creating the appearance that adoption of the changes is voluntary. While consensus is used to make decisions on how some changes will be implemented at a site, others will be standardized across the organization. Opting out is not an option. Therefore, developing a plan of intervention will be critical to maintain a sense of equitable application of the new rules for everyone.

Disruptive behaviors can take many forms. One has to pay attention and respond to those behaviors (just as in any situation) through the enforcement of medical staff bylaws, policies, and procedures; however, in a Lean transformation, one also needs to address what I will call problematic behaviors. Early intervention for these behaviors, which in the past may have only contributed to gossip at coffee breaks, will set a tone that everyone is expected to participate (see Table 6.1).

Problematic behaviors can be part of a constellation of behaviors that are, at times, difficult to identify. They are often not recognized until a nearby observer informs others about the behavior. In addition, it is sometimes not easy to make a decision whether or not to intervene. At times, it may be better to let time, peer feedback, and natural consequences stimulate behavior change. At other times, quick, low-key intervention may be appropriate. What follows are some examples of where tension was created from problematic behavior.

Example 1

One of the difficult but nonnegotiable changes that staff has to make is to 6S their work area in a standard manner. The primary focus for this change is shared workstations; however, if for no other reason than role modeling, physicians, managers, and supervisors are often asked or told to do the same for their work areas. It is particularly important when staff and leaders are co-located in a central area; however, that is frequently not possible because of layout limitations. In those circumstances, if a physician decides to not 6S his/her office, should they be ordered to do so? I've chosen not to force the issue but lead, by example, sharing my story of increased work efficiency from the change. When asked by staff why they have to 6S and the doctors don't, I usually take one of two approaches. One approach is to facilitate the staff asking the physicians

Table 6.1   Disruptive and Problematic Behaviors

Disruptive Behaviors	Problematic Behaviors
Loud angry outbursts at staff or peers	Lack of participation in change efforts
Failure to respond to calls or emergency situations	Lack of adoption of Lean tools and principles
Failure to adhere to hospital or clinic policies	Refusal to speak out when unhappy or disturbed
Use of inappropriate language or humor	Playing favorites
Chronic tardiness in the OR	Failure to adopt standard work
Throwing things (instruments, books, charts, etc.)	Subtle sabotage

directly in a regular Lean meeting. Alternatively, if staff members don't feel comfortable with that approach, I indicate the 6S applies primarily to shared work areas, and we are encouraging the physicians to do the same. Ideally, at least one of the physicians will be intrigued enough to do it and subsequently share the success. I've certainly seen that happen.

Example 2

Two principles of Lean involve team-based care and cross-training staff for many functions. Working environments where there is a 1:1 relationship between a clerical staff person and a physician often require a change to a team-based care model. In this model, everyone chips in to help each other to get work done throughout the day. If a physician plays favorites and insists on only one clinical staff person doing his/her work, an imbalance in the workload invariably results. Level-loading the work (*heijunka*) is another key principle in Lean. Even if, over the course of the day, everyone has the same level of work, the ebb and flow of the workday will result in temporary imbalances in workload. This will ultimately make the workday longer for everyone. One could allow time for the physician to develop trust in the other clinical staff or could intervene quickly if secondary problems are created, producing delays in patient care or staff dissatisfaction.

Example 3

I think some people were "born to batch." Whether it is intuition that batching makes sense or procrastination, some people have a very hard time adopting single piece flow. Staff has no choice but to participate when work flow is changed to single piece flow. For example, look at the instance of changing medical records distribution cycles to 15 minutes as described in Chapter 1. Physicians, on the other hand, are most often the end users of charts, and phone messages gathered to answer patient requests for refills or information. The timely arrival of a prescription refill doesn't necessarily mean the physician will respond to the request in real time. When physicians are batching these requests, it is important to find out how long the requests are being held and whether or not the batching is impacting the patient.

Physicians who adopt single piece flow typically finish their workday sooner than those who batch. It doesn't take long for the batchers to notice their peers leaving earlier. Often, that is all that is needed to accelerate adoption of single piece flow. I know of one case where the physician's clinical assistant used a red/yellow/green card in the area where requests were placed. If a backlog began to build up, she would change the card from green to yellow. If it continued, a red card was placed, with the agreement that the physician would stop at that point and catch up on requests. Eventually, the physician was able to keep the green card all day. If, however, the batching goes beyond a shift or is carried over to the next day, then the patient does have consequences. At that point, an intervention is warranted. I tend to err on the side of giving time for adoption of single piece flow as long as the delay does not impact the patient.

What follows is an example of an intervention plan. It is simply meant to stimulate ideas for what a similar plan might look like at any institution. It is not meant to be viewed as the only way to proceed.

Intervention Plan (Physician Standard Work)
Physician (Clinician) Standard Work
A Lean Perspective

It is important to distinguish between clinical decision-making and the patient care process (see Figure 6.2). In this circumstance, the patient care process refers only to the operational portion of patient care and the working environment. It does not include adherence to clinical guidelines, protocols, and standard clinical orders. Including adherence to clinical protocols along with standard work for the care process is likely to increase resistance and make the work a good deal more complex. I would strongly recommend not including clinical decision making initially in a Lean effort. By including it, a number of new variables would be introduced that would complicate the effort. These would include choosing the "right" protocol, review, and update issues and compliance monitoring. Consequently, I will refer only to the patient care process in the intervention portion in the following text. Outliers as a result of faulty clinical decision making should be dealt with in a standard manner defined by the institution or practice. I don't mean to imply that use of protocols, standing orders, and guidelines should be avoided—only that they should not be included in the Lean effort.

Once the operational patient care process is standardized and efficient, adding individual protocols such as a central line bundle makes a great deal of sense. Indeed, adding a central line bundle to daily rounds (huddles) may increase adoption. Standard work for rounds (huddles) where all members of the care team are assembled could easily include a checklist for the elements of a central line bundle.

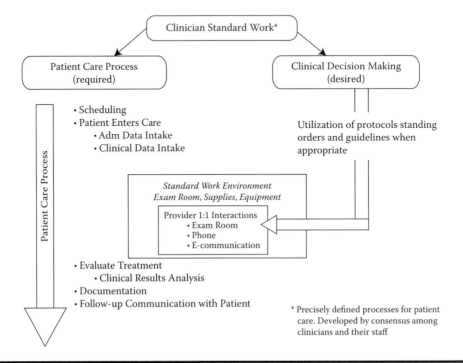

Figure 6.2   Clinician standard work.

Criteria for Intervention

In some cases, adaptation of individual work habits to a Lean environment can take months or even years. In addition, the definition of required behaviors is not always exact. For instance, while single piece flow is the ideal, some batching may be acceptable or even desirable. All would agree that batching charts and Superbills to the end of the day or even the end of a work session is not acceptable; however, batching charts in groups of two or three periodically throughout the day is unlikely to disrupt staff work or pose patient safety problems.

- In general, first efforts to have clinicians adopt standard work should be based on "what's in it for them" and for their patients, accomplished through facilitated consensus decision making on the standards
- Continuous quality improvement using PDCA to constantly improve the standard work over time

The great majority of clinicians will respond to adopt new patient care processes. When that approach is unsuccessful, intervention should occur when:

- Any clinician's patient care process jeopardizes:
  - Timeliness of care (e.g., batching messages, Rx refills, charts, etc.)
  - Patient safety (e.g., variation from standard clinical results notification)
  - Patient satisfaction (e.g., delays in response to patients)
- Work flows for staffing working in the clinic

In other circumstances when these criteria don't apply, continued interaction with a provider to encourage changeover time is appropriate.

Who

- Requests for a change in clinician work habits that are at variance from Lean principles and defined standard work can be initiated by anyone in a particular clinic.
- If unsuccessful, additional requests for change may be through practice administrators, lead physicians, or site Lean teams.
- Continued lack of improvement would escalate to the appropriate associate medical director.
- Final escalation of unsuccessful interventions would be to the executive medical director.

How

- Interventions initially may consist of simple requests or directives for the change.
- If unsuccessful, use of motivational interviewing and gradual change in behavior with monitored progress should be used through Lead physicians or associate medical directors.

If still unsuccessful, intervention with the executive medical director should be done to include discussions of clear expectations and conditions for continued employment.

The necessary elements of an intervention plan include:

- A clear distinction between clinical decision-making and the patient care process
- Guidance for what types of behaviors should stimulate intervention

- Who should intervene
- What type of intervention should be used
- What should trigger escalation

What follows in Chapter 7 are various examples of using this plan during Lean implementations.

Reference

1. Rogers, Everett M. 1995. *Diffusion of Innovations Fourth Edition.* The Free Press, New York.

Chapter 7

Physician Case Studies

The following case studies are for the reader to think about in the context of your own circumstances. I don't believe there is any one right answer to the issues raised. The responses will vary among institutions, depending on the culture and the amount and experience of physician and administrative leadership. I hope, by using the scenarios either individually or in discussions with peers, a sense of a planned approach for a Lean transformation will emerge. Consider these cases from the perspective of a physician leader for a Lean effort being implemented at many different sites. In that case, the leader would not have direct line authority and would have to rely initially on his/her facilitation skills and powers of persuasion.

The term *lead physician* in these scenarios refers to a physician who has leadership responsibility over 8–12 other physicians working in the same area of either a clinic, hospital unit, OR, or ED. I would encourage the reader to reflect on responses to a situation before reading what happened in the actual cases. The actual responses are not meant to be attempts to provide the right answer. They are simply the responses that occurred and represent a wide range of outcomes. After reading, reflect on how to approach these differently.

In some scenarios, slight modifications to the actual events were made to illustrate the intervention impact.

SCENARIO #1

A physician has reluctantly agreed to become a lead physician at a clinic where there hasn't been a lead physician for nearly a year. During the prior year, none of the physicians were willing to be a lead. The acceptance of the position is coincident with the beginning of a Lean implementation. The lead physician's participation and adoption of Lean principles is critical for successful implementation. In the past, the physician has chronically and openly complained about how bad the clinic is and that physicians have to do everything themselves in order to be sure things are done properly. The individual has openly indicated lack of trust in the staff. As the physician leader for Lean in your organization, you led an initial meeting to introduce Lean with the physicians and managers of this location. During the meeting, the lead physician became increasingly upset and angry. At one point, the lead declared "… [the] clinic is fundamentally broken and moving things closer to people, so they don't have to walk as far was not about to fix the problems …." You held private discussions with the physician following the meeting.

Subsequently, the lead physician had several remonstrations during clinic hours that were disturbing for staff and negatively impacted patient flow.

As a leader, you must have an engaged and committed lead physician.

1. How would you initially approach the situation?
2. When there were subsequent behavioral episodes, how would you change your approach?
3. What criteria would you use to judge success?

SCENARIO #2

Coincident with a Lean implementation in a large multispecialty clinic, a physician has covertly started sabotaging the effort. During group meetings, the physician never speaks negatively or positively about the Lean concepts and the implementation process. During a meeting where a consensus decision was made by physicians and staff about standard work for distribution of messages and charts, this individual was silent. The staff subsequently placed trays and labels for "in/out/urgent communications" in physicians' offices. Each day, the staff would come in and find the labels and trays removed and the physician office rearranged to pre-Lean status. They would restore the office to the Lean standards, only to face the same problem the next day. Similar behavior was exhibited around exam room standardization. When questioned, the physician denied any problems and indicated that his exam rooms weren't used by anyone else and did not need to be standard. The physician had exhibited similar behaviors in other settings. For instance, this individual refused to refer patients to the diabetes educators who were part of the on-site diabetes team.

As a leader, you must have engagement, commitment, and participation from all the physicians in the clinic. The clinic has a lead physician.

1. After being informed of the circumstances, what would be your initial approach?
2. If, after a period of time, there did not seem to be any improvement, what approach would you use?

SCENARIO #3

In a clinic, a new communication/lab test follow-up process was developed by staff and a team of physicians using a Plan-Do-Check-Act (PDCA) methodology. The old system relied on printed results, at times in duplicate and triplicate. Previously, follow-up was accomplished by reviewing copies of previously ordered lab tests to make sure they were completed and reported. The new plan involved electronic follow-up and reporting. The changes demonstrated greater safety, efficiency, reduced paper consumption, and shortened cycle time for patients to receive results.

This physician refused to have the nurse participate in the new process. When asked why, the individual replied that he would be the one sued if results were missed, not the staff. "…. One time in the past a result was missed for over 3 weeks for one [of this physician's] patient." With meticulous attention to detail by the physician and nurse, they could demonstrate similar results as those from the new process adopted by all others in the clinic; however, they had to spend a large amount of time on the task that others in the clinic now (with the new method) could devote to other needed activities.

As a leader, you must have engagement, commitment, and participation from all the physicians in the clinic.

1. What would your initial response be to this circumstance?
2. What sort of follow-up would you use to monitor the situation?

SCENARIO #4

Early on a Monday morning a clinic manager "caught" a physician unloading 54 charts from the trunk of a car and loading them onto a cart to be returned to medical records at the site. The legal department of your institution has repeatedly reminded physicians, staff, and managers of the risk associated with temporary removal of medical records from clinics. It is a forbidden practice, although "everyone knows that physicians take a few charts home at night on an occasional basis to catch up." When approached, the physician replied that he was already staying until 9–10 at night trying to get required work and documentation completed. The physician was not willing to spend additional time working in the clinic in order to complete all the documentation requirements.

As a leader, you must have engagement, commitment, and participation from all the physicians in the clinic.

1. After the manager informs you of the discovery, what would your initial approach be?
2. What follow-up approach would you use?

SCENARIO #5

On a busy Friday night in the ED, a catheterization was ordered for a male patient. The recently changed work flows called for the patient to be moved to a designated procedure room for the catheterization. The nurse felt moving the patient would be unnecessary work. The nurse was good at catheterizations and insisted on doing the procedure in the exam room. Rather than confront the nurse and refuse the request, the physician allowed the catheterization to take place in the exam room. Of course, Murphy's law prevailed; the catheterization was difficult, requiring multiple attempts by three different people. The patient occupied the exam room for a prolonged period of time, resulting in a backup in patient flow.

Afterward, the physician called the team together to discuss what everyone had learned and reinforced the need to follow the new work flow.

1. You hear about the episode a week later. What would be your approach?

SCENARIO #6

Long turn-around times and late starts were the norm in the OR. The surgeon routinely had time after the scheduled start of a case for a cup of coffee and visits with peers in the lounge before he had to show up in the operating room. During the Lean implementation, new work flows for turn-around times resulted in dramatic reductions in cycle times. Almost overnight, the physician became the obstacle for an on-time start time. The patient, room, and staff were routinely ready on time and waiting for the surgeon to arrive. In spite of the change, the surgeon continued to take time for coffee and visit with peers, resulting in a late start time for his cases. The surgeon's cases were among those scheduled first thing in the day.

1. After a couple of weeks of this pattern persisting, you are informed of the situation during a routine weekly Lean meeting. What is your initial approach?
2. How will you monitor and follow-up on the situation?

SCENARIO #7

New work flows were developed in the ED to separate low- from high-acuity patients into different value streams. Patients were to be triaged on arrival into the appropriate work flow for either low or high acuity. Equitable schedules were developed by the physicians to spend time in both work flows. The low-acuity work flows were designed to work with a higher number of patients per hour than previously occurred when the patients were mixed in the same work flow. One physician refused to work in the low-acuity, higher-volume fast track. He indicated that he could not work that fast and still provide good care.

1. The lead physician has tried unsuccessfully to get the physician to increase patients seen per hour. How would you approach the situation?
2. What sort of follow-up and monitoring would you put in place?

SCENARIO #8

A lead physician was an outspoken opponent of Lean in the early phases of an implementation. Intervention was accomplished to help the lead at least portray a positive attitude. As improvements began to occur in the location, the lead physician gradually began to recognize Lean as contributing to the greater good of the site. Near the end of the implementation, the lead was an outspoken supporter of Lean and the improvements that occurred at the site. The lead often spoke in casual conversations about initially being a skeptic but now becoming a believer in Lean.

1. How would you approach this situation?

Discussion

Scenario #1

Initial informal private meetings were held when the lead physician had a break. Key problems from the lead's perspective were elicited and discussed, with a commitment to check in on those problems and progress toward resolution. The lead was also asked to be less oppositional and to give Lean a chance to address some of the identified problems.

Subsequently there were fewer negative public comments about Lean. Later, when a new test of change was proposed. The lead physician was opposed, exhibited strong staunch protest and threatened to refuse to participate. This behavior was deemed a threat to the overall successful implenention of the Lean effort. To address the behavior a meeting was scheduled with the lead physician, medical director for Lean and the executive medical director for the group. During that meeting mutual expectations for future behavior for both the lead physician and the lean team were developed and agreed upon. As a result the laed physician even started making public comments about giving Lean a chance.

Shortly thereafter, improvements from the Lean effort began to occur that dramatically improved some of the problems initially described by the lead. Other problems continued to be included in a project priority matrix posted in the Lean work room as visual evidence that the other problems were not forgotten.

Eventually, the lead became an outspoken proponent of Lean and made presentations to other sites in the system, the quality committee of the board, and even public venues.

Scenario #2

In this circumstance, there was no intervention by the Lean team. The problems manifest in all settings and did not seem specifically related to the Lean effort. Multiple attempts by the lead physician and others in the oversight positions were not successful. The physician is no longer with the organization.

Scenario #3

The physician was approached and asked what it would take to prove to him that the new system was safe, effective, and timely. Initially, the response was negative and that the labs would continue to be monitored as in the past. In spite of this, accuracy data was presented to the physician on a weekly basis showing the superior results with the electronic monitoring. Eventually, the physician recognized it was not equitable or a good use of the nurse's time to follow the old method. The nurse was allowed to use the new tracking system; however, the physician did continue to use a personal notebook to monitor and follow-up labs on his own.

Scenario #4

In this case, the physician was reminded of the rules about charts and the resulting consequences if litigation occurred; however, there was a recognition that the need for the physician to have to stay very late in the clinic was inappropriate. A temporary agreement was made that the physician would not take charts home, pending attempts at improvement by the Lean team. It wasn't long before the physician was able to complete needed documentation and routinely leave work within 30 minutes of seeing the last patient.

Scenario #5

Every attempt should be made to recognize this physician's approach to the situation as being ideal. The physician was recognized in several venues, and the methodology used was discussed to help others when faced with similar situations. The physician assessed the situation, allowed the change, monitored the results, and debriefed on the results. It was decided to not change the standard work. Sound like PDCA?

Had the physician simply refused, there would probably have been no further learning, and it would have likely created some resentment. The staff involved now had a better understanding of the rationale for moving the patient for a procedure because of how the physician chose to handle it.

The physician should be recognized as a potential candidate for further leadership roles in future Lean efforts.

Scenario #6

There was no intervention by the Lean team. Staff began to publicly post start times (unblinded) in the OR for room time, anesthesia, physician, etc. The surgeon began showing up more promptly for the cases.

Scenario #7

This was felt to be an issue of clinical care competence and productivity. Lean is designed to create greater throughput of patients, but it should not be because physicians are to see patients at a greater rate than they are competent to function. In fact, ideally, physicians should have more time to spend with patients.

The problem was left in the hands of the department and associate medical director of the group. A meeting was held to indicate that working in fast track at a reasonable speed was going to be required. Visit rates per hour for all ED physicians were tracked by the group. In addition, support was offered to address the cycle times for patients seen in the ED by the physician. Ideas were shared for how other physicians were able to see more low-acuity patients in the same amount of time. The physician was able to adapt over time.

Scenario #8

The physician was recognized for the support. She was also asked to address others in the medical group, the quality committee of the board, and was even a spokesperson on a local TV show. The lead's impact from changed behavior was dramatic, and the site became one of the most successful.

From these examples, it should be apparent that a physician leader for a Lean transformation will require a full portfolio of intervention strategies. The portfolio includes, among other choices, watchful waiting, leveraging peer pressure, a good sense of when to use data publicly, gentle persuasion, motivation, and creating or imposing consequences. She should have the skill set and experience to use a wide array of approaches.

Chapter 8

Keys to Sustaining Lean—A Physician Guide

There are two early findings associated with a successful Lean deployment. First, all the steps of a deployment are completed in a prescribed timeline. Second, some process outcomes are achieved. Results (financial, quality, satisfaction) may not follow for several months after the implementation began (see Figure 8.1). For instance, early in a clinic transformation, one might see improvements in patient visit and prescription refill cycle times. Some period of time may follow before patient satisfaction improves, and reduced FTEs and associated cost savings appear. Alternatively, on a hospital ward, reduced length of stay may show up early and be followed months later by improved financial performance secondary to increased throughput and decreased cost. The lag time between the start-up phase and when a positive impact on net revenue occurs will vary by location and circumstance. I think improvements in quality outcomes and patient satisfaction are less predictable in terms of when they may first appear but may take as long as 12–18 months.

A successful Lean implementation is foundational for the gains to be sustained in the future. There are some key success factors and possible failure points that one needs to be aware of.

1. *Before beginning an implementation, an assessment of the number and complexity of improvement initiatives planned for the location needs to be accomplished.* Known as an *energy grid*, it is vital that an assessment be made of the amount of change staff and physicians are going to have to deal with during the implementation. If there are already a number of change initiatives happening, it will make success more difficult to achieve and will result in less than desired outcomes.

   During one implementation, for example, organizational needs outweighed the need to keep demands for change to a manageable level. A call center initiative that isolated operators from the local site, the nursing model change to a team-based configuration, and a Lean implementation were all started at the same time. Shortly after the Lean implementation began, there was also a change in management configuration. The resulting chaos was difficult to manage and even began to affect the Lean implementation team, resulting in gaps

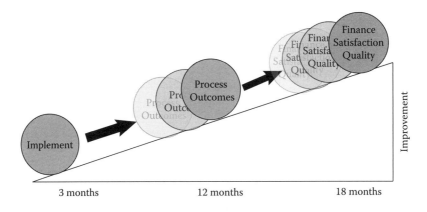

Figure 8.1   Progression of improvement outcomes.

in execution of Lean principles. The outcomes were limited to a few tools (some 6S, Kanban) and minimal culture change (some huddles).

2. *Enough time should be allotted for the needed cultural changes to be assimilated by staff, physicians, managers, and leaders.* Individuals and organizations tend to focus on just the tools. David Mann indicates that only 20% of successful outcomes are attributable to tools, while 80% is dependent on culture change.[1] I believe cultural adaptation is the rate limiting factor during the implementation phase. If people don't have time to understand and adopt the new culture, sustainment is very unlikely.

    I don't know the exact minimum time for cultural adaptation to happen. I have tried a 60-day implementation in a small specialty practice. The staff, management, and physicians did not have time to adopt the culture change. Soon after the implementation team left the clinic, old habits and work patterns quickly reemerged. With a 120-day implementation, there is ample time for individuals to begin adapting to the new culture. Any less time allocated than 100 days can result in skipped steps and leave other steps uncompleted. Artificial attempts to accelerate timelines because of organizational impatience have, in my experience, resulted in disappointing results. Conversely, in large departments (e.g., operating suites), there may be implementations occurring for months or even years.

3. *A detailed plan of implementation and associated timeline should be shared with everyone at the site.* People will need to be able to track progress as the implementation proceeds. The plan and timeline should be referred to at least weekly to make sure the implementation is on time and on track.

4. *Be alert for organizational Lean "just do it" mandates.* Organizations will be very tempted to try and take a successful change at one site and mandate the change at other sites. While the change may be appropriate, bypassing the analysis and "buy-in" by staff at another site in an attempt to accelerate spread will make sustaining the effort extremely difficult. It may even create unintended resistance to other Lean efforts. Mandates are sometimes successful in the short run but are frequently not sustainable.

5. *Value stream mapping (VSM) should be performed through direct observation and measurement.* A VSM should not be constructed in a meeting room relying solely on individuals' recollections of a particular process. Doing so will invariably lead to omissions and lost opportunities to improve. One possible exception to this is where Lean implementations are being deployed at several similar sites. For instance, in primary care clinics in a single

organization, it may work to simply validate a previous VSM from another primary care clinic. The validation should still be done by direct observation and measurement, but it will take less time to complete than starting a VSM from scratch.

6. *A training schedule and plan should be implemented as follows:*

   a. Training should occur for all staff on basic Lean tools and principles such as 6S, Kanban, single piece flow, standard work, etc.

   b. Training sessions should also include teaching all staff about the improvement model and expectations for process improvement teams.

   c. Managers and leaders will need extensive training/work sessions to learn and understand how to operate in a Lean culture. Ninety-five percent of managers and supervisors do not have a master's degree in either business or healthcare administration.[2] They typically have come up through the ranks and have learned their approaches and skills on the job. Consequently, the overwhelming majority of these managers practice what is called "modern" or "traditional" management approaches, which are learned from others in the organization. They may not have had any exposure to new management approaches.

   They will need to learn new skills to be successful in a Lean environment. Managers and supervisors will also need to be coached on how to begin making the transition. It will not be easy for many of them. They will have to make more changes in how they work than anyone else in the organization to be successful in a Lean environment. It is not surprising that the highest turnover rate during a Lean transition is among managers and supervisors. A strong commitment through training and coaching will help minimize turnover for these valuable leaders.

   d. Change management should be taught to administrative leaders, managers, and supervisors in addition to physician leaders. Change management training will introduce new methods and approaches for preventing, recognizing, and responding to resistance.

7. *Expect some significant acting out from staff as well as physicians.* It may seem odd to list "acting out behavior" as a key success factor. If it does not occur at some level, one should explore whether the intensity and depth of the implementation is great enough to ensure successful outcomes. When undergoing change of the magnitude involved with Lean, peoples' worst behaviors will come to the surface. You will likely see overt and covert acts of sabotage.

   I've observed acts of sabotage that included destroying materials related to Lean in meeting rooms and obscene graffiti in bathrooms. One episode involved one of the medical assistants who volunteered to become a "water spider" (a term for the person who goes around and restocks equipment and materials once a Kanban system is in place.) She jokingly told her fellow workers that everything had better be the same (labels, locations of supplies, etc.) when she came back from her vacation. The physician she worked with was also on vacation. When she returned, she found all the drawers and cabinets in her exam rooms filled with vaginal speculums instead of the required equipment and materials.

   Behavioral outbursts and screaming at one another is also not uncommon. These behaviors should never be condoned or ignored and should be dealt with promptly; however, if one is not seeing some of these behaviors occur for a short while, the effectiveness and intensity of the Lean implementation should be questioned.

   Typically, they occur around 3–4 weeks into an implementation during what is euphemistically known as "the valley of despair." This is the period when people actually have to change their work environment and how they work. They recognize that this is not going away and that they are truly going to have to change. It should not last in any significant way beyond another 3–4 weeks. At that point, most people have accepted the new reality and are engaged in figuring out how to be successful.

8. *A plan for physician input and participation should be developed and in place from the beginning of the implementation.* Failure to do so will result in inconsistent results and islands of nonconformity. All the physicians at a location should be given the plan and asked to review it. If there are disagreements with the plan, they should be surfaced at the very beginning.

    Dr. John Toussaint in his book *On the Mend: Revolutionizing Healthcare to Save Lives and Transform the Industry* states there are several key approaches when interacting with physicians:
    a. Never lie.
    b. Be willing to admit management mistakes.
    c. Ask for opinions and take their advice seriously.
    d. Be forthright about intentions.
    e. Be clear about the process of care delivery and how it needs to work.

9. *Ownership of the Lean process and culture should always lie with the managers and supervisors at the local level.* However, in the beginning of an implementation process, they are poorly equipped to manage and lead the effort. During the implementation, they will become more knowledgeable and subsequently able to lead the process. Initially, the organizational Lean team will typically direct the process. Over time they should coach and mentor local leaders to assume more and more responsibility for the Lean process and maintaining a Lean culture. If not, when the organizational Lean team leaves the site, the effort will collapse and people will revert to old work habits.

    In my experience, we had some success with transitioning the responsibility for presenting information on progress at periodic toll gate (review) meetings. At these meetings, senior leaders and organizational Lean teams from a particular site would review their progress toward meeting benchmarks and timelines. Initially, these presentations would be made by the organizational Lean team. With each succeeding tollgate (usually three), the managers and supervisors took more responsibility for presenting the material and answering questions. By the final session, they would be totally responsible for the sessions with the organizational Lean team acting only as backup.

10. *Near the end of an implementation phase, one should be seeing visual evidence of the Lean effort.* Visual controls should be prominently displayed and actively maintained. The telephone availability graph (Chapter 1) maintained by the telephone operators regarding their availability to answer the phone would be a good example. The day-by-hour chart (Chapter 1) for the PACU is another example. Red, yellow, and green indicators to indicate whether a backlog is building up that needs someone's attention may be appropriate. For processes that have been determined to be critical for efficient operations, there should be some sort of indicator that people can see to reflect current status. If one does not see visual controls, the Lean effort may not be sustainable.

11. *By the end of the implementation phase, standard work for all key job positions should be in place and posted for people to see and quickly access.* It is important for the individual worker, but also very important to supervisors, managers, and physicians. Remember the case study of the ED physician (Chapter 2) who used standard work to reinforce the rationale for a care process of doing procedures in one room, so it did not interrupt patient flow. That physician had to know or have ready access to that standard work. Posting standard work is a key factor in reinforcing to everyone that this is how we want work to be performed.

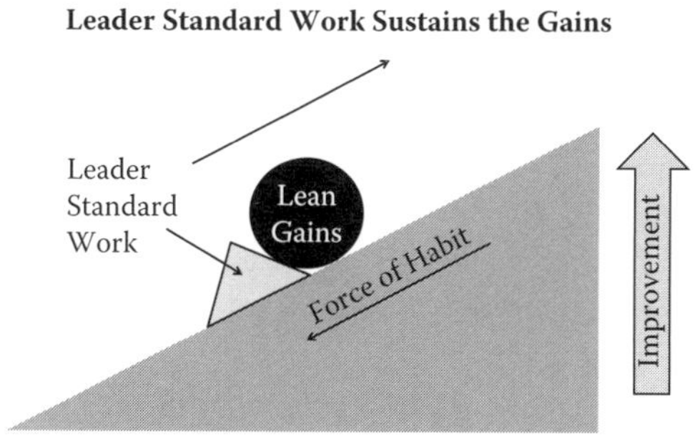

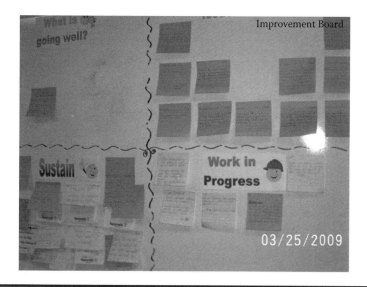

Figure 8.2   Leader standard work. (Reprinted with permission. Illustration by Scott Simmons.)

Figure 8.3   Improvement board.

12. *Standard work for leaders is of particular importance.* Without a defined routine that managers and supervisors can be held accountable to, work processes performed by the staff will begin to deteriorate quickly (see Figure 8.2). People will begin to drift back to their old habits. Regression to old habits acts like the earth's gravitational pull away from change, innovation, and improvement. *The primary mitigating force is well-executed standard work for leaders, managers, and supervisors.* In addition, the leaders must execute the standard work through *gemba* walks in a reliable fashion every day. The *gemba* walks may include the use of assessment tools as well as simple observations and conversations with staff about problems and improvement ideas. The assessments must not just include a checklist, but a thorough review of visual controls, process analysis, and improvement plans when gaps are found.

In addition, managers should have daily huddles around a quality improvement progress board (see Figure 8.3). These boards are used to manage and monitor identified problems, and improvement project status. They typically contain sections for:

What is going well?

Issues/problems

Improvement project ideas/development

Improvement projects in progress

Projects in the sustain phase

Managers should review each section of the board daily along with key staff members. If new problems and new improvement ideas are not forthcoming, the manager should take action to regenerate new ideas.

13. *Daily huddles should be occurring at the beginning of the day or beginning of shift work.* To reemphasize, huddles should be stand-up sessions of 5 minutes or less. Attendees should include most, if not all, of the personnel working in the local area. Huddles should be organized everywhere. They might be for a specialty clinic or pod in a larger clinic, a hospital ward, ED, urgent care, or operating room.

Huddles are typically organized around a huddle board. Huddle boards are meant to visually communicate to everyone what improvement projects are active and what progress is being made. Anyone walking by could see what current issues and projects are occurring. Some organizations even postpatient, staff, and physician satisfaction on huddle boards (see Figure 8.4).

Standard work for huddles (Table 8.1) should be developed and used in a uniform way throughout the organization.

Attention to these 12 items and avoiding known pitfalls (see Table 8.2) will help ensure a stable long-term outcome. Now, the focus shifts to roles and responsibilities for people at the site once the core Lean team leaves.

14. *One member of the organizational team should stay behind at the site for 2–4 weeks after the implementation phase, depending on the maturity of the site leadership to coach and mentor those who will be carrying on the effort locally.* The immediate period of time when the organizational Lean team leaves a site is particularly vulnerable to regression to old habits. The

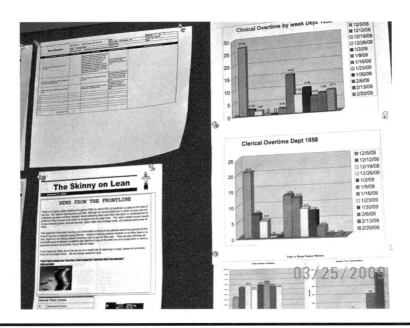

Figure 8.4   Huddle board.

Table 8.1   Huddle Board Standard Work

Gather Staff Around Huddle Board	Specify a Consistent Time for Huddle Each Day	Builds Team Structure
Ask the first question— What's going well?	Opportunity to capture positive activities, positive feedback, and create opportunity for real-time recognition of team members	Part of organizational rounding
Daily/weekly huddle topics	Potential topics: (1) review staff resources available, (2) plan staffing based on number of providers, (3) review schedules to identify special needs patients and identify appropriate slots to provide additional access for sick calls, (4) develop plan for lunch breaks	Opportunity to discuss work to do based on staffing and to develop staffing strategy based on future PTO.
IDEA: Ideas generated for improvement by frontline team members. Discuss ideas for continuous improvement—work the board.	Frontline staff to determine which top three ideas move to the "to do" section of the huddle board. Assign date and champion/owner of the project/task. Provide feedback on status of ideas in implementation	Engage staff in taking ownership of idea implementation. Important for staff to know their ideas are valued
To do	To do: Ideas assigned a project name but not champion or process owner	Review "to do" ideas every 7 days to ensure ideas continue to be acted on and if an idea is able to be moved to sustain on Management Continuous Improvement Board.
SUSTAIN:	SUSTAIN: (1) Just-do-it projects that all team members have agreed upon and implemented. (2) Process projects implemented that have assessments showing it has become a habit.	Process has become a habit, has appropriate measures/ assessments in place, and has been communicated to the team at the all-team Lean meeting to validate success.

Table 8.2 Pitfalls to Avoid

Pitfalls to Avoid
In the following are some of the most common sources of failure, many of which have been introduced earlier in this chapter. By understanding these sources of difficulty and proactively working to avoid them, you can dramatically increase the success of your improvement efforts.
1. Treating the project as single event as opposed to long-term commitment to change.
2. Lack of top-down management support—senior management reinforcing key principles.
3. Preparing management and the organization for SUSTAIN, including metrics, adherence, reporting, and tracking. Systems and structure include upgrading job descriptions and performance evaluations reflecting expectations in the new lean environment.
4. Lack of middle-management/supervisor buy-in (not role modeling).
5. Focusing on the wrong things.
6. Not dealing with resistance.
7. Lack of customer and value stream focus.
8. Not combining standard work with Kaizen.
9. Lack of clear performance measures.
10. Over-reliance on a tool or tools (Kaizen, Kanban, 5S).
11. Quick leaps to "lean doesn't work here."
12. Pointing the finger at everyone else first—"We are fine; the real problem is …."
13. Inadequate partnering with support services.
14. Dysfunction of teams (core, site, frontline staff).
15. The most significant failure mode that is completely within your control is not understanding Lean yourself.

team members remaining with the site should not be personally doing any of the Lean work. Rather the person should be there to help others, understand and carry out their standard work as well as improvement initiatives.

At this point, leader standard work including daily *gemba* walks and improvement board huddles should be well established. Visual controls should be in place and data about progress produced regularly. In Chapter 10, the transition to and the maintenance of the sustainment phase are reviewed.

References

1. Mann, David. 2005. *Creating a Lean Culture.* New York: Productivity Press.
2. Toussaint, John, Gerard, Roger A., and Adams, Emily, on the Mend: Revolutionizing Health Care to Save Lives and Transform the Industry, Cambridge: Lean Enterprise Institute, Inc., 2010.

Chapter 9

Judging Lean Success
The Process

Developing consensus about the relative degree of success from a Lean transformation can be a vexing problem. There are a rather large number of factors that, at any given time, can impact the results obtained during a Lean transformation and obscure causality for the outcome. These include the various factors that can impact operational performance and the unique perspectives of various constituencies that will judge whether the effort was successful (see Figure 9.1).

The perceptions and beliefs of the different constituencies who have a stake in the outcomes can be quite different from one another. Board members may have different perspectives than the finance department or human resources. People working at a given location who are primarily interested in their working conditions may have yet another perspective. An individual's needs, wants, desires, and beliefs will shape perceptions about the relative success of a Lean effort (see Table 9.1).

At any given point in time, there are almost always different business activities and market forces occurring that make it very difficult to isolate Lean as a causative factor in a given outcome. Workforce reductions, freezes on spending, or, conversely, expansion of new facilities will of course impact financial and workplace efficiency in addition to any Lean effort occurring at the same time. Because of all these factors that can simultaneously impact outcomes, it is important for an organization embarking on a Lean transformation to have predeployment discussions regarding how they will judge success.

Perceptions about success will largely drive continued organizational investment in future Lean activities. Consequently, the ability to sustain is heavily dependent on consensus about Lean outcomes in the first few years. Ultimately, most organizations require a financial return on investment (ROI).

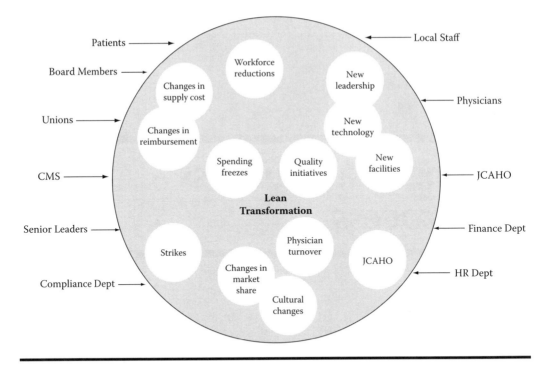

Figure 9.1 Environmental factors impacting lean success.

Financial Success

One of the most difficult areas to reach consensus about is how to measure and judge financial outcomes. Fortunately, there are now alternatives to traditional accounting practices that are more helpful in a Lean environment.[1–5]

Alfred P. Sloan has been called the most advanced practitioner of modern management of our time. He was responsible for teaching and training thousands of managers the principles of modern management.

> Much has been written about the folly of using financial equations to drive decision making, but it is the legacy handed down from Sloan in the form of modern management that has proved to be the single biggest impediment to lean healthcare.[1]

I have no expertise in accounting or finance; however, I have witnessed the conflicts that can occur and the opportunities that can be overlooked when traditional finance and accounting principles are used for ROI to predict financial success. I also believe that some very worthy projects will be ignored if a hard-dollar ROI is a prerequisite for approval. I have witnessed the folly that sometimes occurs when trying to reach an artificial hurdle of proving a hard-dollar ROI in order to get approval for a project. I don't think most traditional accounting systems have the capacity to produce accurate reports at that granular level.

> Companies that begin the transition from batch and queue to Lean manufacturing always run into problems with accounting systems, with the biggest issue

Table 9.1 Constituent Interests

Constituency	Outcome Focus
• Patients	• Improved cycle times (office visits, Rx refills, etc.) • Improved access • Affordability • Service
• Board of governors	• Sound financial performance • Quality outcomes
• Senior leaders	• Lowered cost-improved margins • Quality outcomes • Workforce stability
• Physicians	• Operational efficiency • Improved productivity • A chance to have input
• HR department	• Decreased turnover • Increased employee satisfaction
• Finance department	• Hard dollar return on investment
• Staff	• A chance to do meaningful work • Workplace efficiency • Employee satisfaction

being cost accounting. As teams of employees tear out old processes, move equipment, cut waste, and continue to do this over time, determining the cost of any one product becomes difficult. In fact, it becomes more frustrating with each improvement.

Jean Cunningham and Orest Fiume
Real Numbers Management Accounting in a Lean Organization[1]

Attempting to determine the cost of a patient-care process like a hospitalization can be a challenge in the traditional finance world. Traditional cost accounting practices can lead to false assumptions about financial outcomes secondary to being departmental based rather than process based.

> Value stream costing (VSC) supports Lean thinking and continuous improvement in the value stream. Traditional management accounting methods are usually actively hostile to Lean manufacturing because they encourage and reinforce non-Lean behaviors. VSC eliminates the need for these wasteful and misleading traditional systems.

The Lean Business Management System[2]

Lean is focused on the patient care process (value stream), which flows horizontally across departmental divisions. Improvements in outcomes sometimes appear in areas of the organization that are remote from the department where the initiative occurred. For instance, an improvement in lab test turnaround times might have a profound effect on physician and nursing time on the various units. If results are available during morning rounds, fewer callbacks and time spent trying to track down results will result in significant labor savings. It is a challenge when using traditional accounting methods to validate this scenario.

When using traditional cost accounting practices, it helps to focus more on the macro-level finances than the micro level. It is when hard dollar return on investment is used to judge return on investment (ROI) at the individual project level that outcomes become more difficult to interpret.

For instance, in the case study that follows in Chapter 10, there were many environmental factors (micro view) that could, and probably did, have an impact on the overall improvement in net margin. Organization-wide spending freezes, position control, and physician turnover, all occurred during the period of time in the case study. However, the one distinction for this clinic is that it was the first and most advanced Lean implementation among 15 primary care clinics. None of the other clinics experienced the same degree of financial improvement during the same time period (macro view), a fact that should have a significant impact when judging success.

A Balanced Approach

Consensus should be developed around when to measure and what to measure at different times. The when to measure question is a bit of an oxymoron because Lean is a continuous journey requiring reassessment on a constant basis. Success implies the end of a journey that does not occur in a Lean culture; however, how you measure and what you measure may change at different points in time. There are, I believe, three basic elements of a monitoring system each potentially deployed at different times and in different combinations. They include (1) tollgates, (2) in-person monitoring, and (3) scorecards.

Tollgates

Tollgate reviews should be used early in the process of creating a Lean transformation. They are typically attended by the core (organizational) Lean team, site Lean team, managers, lead physician, and representative senior leaders. The reviews should be constructed to show completeness and timeliness at different stages of an implementation. For instance, a natural tollgate review would be at the end of the analysis phase of an implementation, asking whether the VSM, labor analysis, full work analysis, and baseline metrics were established, and what were the results. At a later point, review of the execution of Lean tools such as 6S, Kanban, and single piece flow would be appropriate for another tollgate. Culture transformation should be woven through all the tollgates, primarily manifested by the ability of the leaders, managers, and supervisors to have more and more accountability for leading the tollgate sessions.

In-Person Monitoring

Near the end of the implementation phase, more *gemba* walks should start occurring along with the assessments around standard work and execution of Lean principles/tools (e.g., 6S,

Kanban). These should be conducted by managers and supervisors and those leaders to whom they report. The results should be reviewed at the site by a leadership team that includes the lead physician. To the extent possible, Lead physicians should also participate in *gemba* walks. In addition to the *gemba* walks, there should be some oversight for the overall number and quality of improvement projects occurring at any one point in time for a site. If the number of improvement projects is declining, indicating people are running out of improvement ideas, the effort should be revitalized, either through management suggestions for improvement projects or staff meetings, to uncover new ideas. Thedacare in their outpatient clinics has a daily report which lists items that must be accomplished each day. If those are happening, they believe they will achieve the outcomes they want. Each morning the reports are reviewed centrally and, if something is missing, the clinic is contacted immediately to determine what help they need to get back on track.[5]

Scorecards

Traditional systemwide scorecards start with content that aligns with the organization's vision, mission, strategies, and goals. These typically cascade down to a local clinic, hospital, or other entity in an aligned fashion. Lean measures don't always fit in with the systemwide balanced scorecard measures. I recommend keeping a separate Lean scorecard directly focused on the outcomes that would be expected from a Lean implementation. These scorecards should cascade in a fashion that is similar to system scorecards. An example of a Lean scorecard is included in Figure 9.2. This scorecard is organized around the stakeholders and expected outcomes for a Lean transformation. The scorecard is populated with both process and outcome measures. Included are these site-specific categories

- Clinical outcomes
- Financial outcomes
- Patient focus
- Provider (physician) focus
- Staff focus

Clinical outcomes can be tailored to the primary work performed at a site. Potential examples are included in Table 9.2

For patients, the three areas of focus are overall satisfaction, telephone, and appointment access. Patients may also be interested in office visit and prescription refill cycle times. All of these are amenable to process improvement tactics using Lean methodology. Focus groups with patients might be used to determine which measures to track.

Financial measures include net margin to budget, but the cost indicators are measured against productivity in the form of relative value units (RVU). If one were to measure just cost, there would be too many variables at play, including changes in provider numbers as a result of turnover.

For providers, the primary focus is on satisfaction, productivity, and throughput in the form of patients seen per hour in this example for a clinic. In the hospital, throughput measures could include average length of stay (ALOS) or total volume of patients for a given period of time. Physicians may be uncomfortable with measuring patients per hour. There is usually a period of disbelief when initial results are revealed. For instance, it is not uncommon to have rates as low as 1.5–2 patients per hour in the ED and some outpatient clinics. It is a measure that is very

BALANCED LEAN SCORECARD

Clinical Outcomes	Freq	Current Actual	Current Target	Better or (Worse) than Target	Yr End Target
Diabetes A1c in Good Control (PMG)	M				
Coumadin Anticoagulation Percent of Results In Range	M				

Customer Loyalty	Freq	Current Actual	Current Target	Better or (Worse) than Target	Yr End Target
Press Ganey - Patient Satisfaction (Percentile)	Q				
TSF (answer within 30 sec)	M				
Abandonment Rate - Telephone	M				
Percent Available - Telephone	M				
Access 3rd next available(in days) ↓	M				

Financial Outcomes	Freq	Current Actual	Current Target	Better or (Worse) than Target	Yr End Target
Margin to Budget	Q				
Supply Cost per Work RVU (rolling 12 months) ↓	M				
Labor Cost per Work RVU (rolling 12 months) ↓	M				
Total Cost per Work RVU (rolling 12 months) ↓	M				

Provider Focus: Productivity & Satisfaction	Freq	Current Actual	Current Target	Better or (Worse) than Target	Yr End Target
TBD physician satisfaction question					
% productivity for Physicians (MGMA)	M				
RVU per FTE Provider	M				
Avg Appointments completed / provider / hour					

Staff Focus: Lean Culture	Freq	Current Actual	Current Target	Better or (Worse) than Target	Yr End Target
Work teams actively problem solve without needing to involve management.	Q				
Management responds quickly to my needs and suggestions.	Q				
Every person receiving care at this clinic experiences a consistent patient care experience.	Q				

Figure 9.2 Balanced Lean scorecard.

amenable to Lean methodologies and improves quickly as Lean efficiencies are achieved. The results should be handled in a nonjudgmental learning fashion.

The staff focus is about measuring whether a Lean culture has been established at the site. The particular questions on this scorecard were selected from the Lean survey presented earlier in the book. Staff satisfaction on this particular scorecard was not used secondary to infrequent (annual) sampling. One could certainly also include overall employee satisfaction.

Scorecards are lagging indicators, meaning that if you wait to rely on results on a scorecard to indicate there may be problems, you are probably too late, and a good deal of damage or backtracking has already occurred. If the first two elements are accomplished successfully, only relative degrees of success—and never negative results—should show up on a scorecard. It would be a mistake to

Table 9.2   Potential Measures to use with a Lean scorecard.

Location	Measures
• ICU	• Central line infections • Ventilator-associated pneumonia
• OR	• Antibiotic administration • Preoperative infections
• ED	• Door-to-balloon time • Blood culture prior to antibiotics for community acquired pneumonia
• Long-term care	• Falls • Skin ulcers
• Hospital unit	• Pneumovax administration • Beta blocker prior to discharge

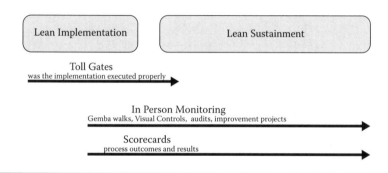

Figure 9.3   Monitoring strategies for sustaining Lean.

rely solely on a scorecard to provide reassurance that all is functioning well. The use of all three elements is also a critical foundation for successfully sustaining the Lean process (Figure 9.3).

References

1. John Toussaint, Roger A. Gerard, and Emily Adams. *On the Mend: Revolutionizing Health Care to Save Lives and Transform the Industry.* Cambridge: Lean Enterprise Institute, Inc.
2. Jean E. Cunningham and Orest J. Fiume. *Real Numbers: Management Accounting in a Lean Organization.* Durham: Managing Times Press, 2003.
3. Brian Maskell et al. *The Lean Business Management System: Lean Accounting: Principles and Practices Toolkit.* Cherry Hill: BMA, Inc., 2007.
4. Brian H. Maskell and Bruce Baggalcy. *Practical Lean Accounting: A Proven System for Measuring and Managing the Lean Enterprise.* New York: Productivity Press, 2003.
5. Jerrod M. Solomon. *Who's Counting? A Lean Accounting Business Novel.* Fort Wayne: WCM Associates, 2003.
6. Thedacare workshop on office redesign. *IHI 8th Annual Summit on Redesigning the Office Practice.* March 27, 2007.

Chapter 10

A Case Study

The clinic is a primary care office with nine physicians in pediatrics, internal medicine, and family practice. It is located in a lower socioeconomic area and serves patients of a variety of ethnic backgrounds; however, the majority of patients have insurance either through the private sector or governmental programs. It is part of an integrated system with hospitals and a health plan, and has been open a little more than 10 years. The physicians are employed by the system and are paid on a productivity basis. In January 2008, when we first started Lean, patient satisfaction goals had never been met, morale was low with high turnover, and the clinic routinely lost more than a million dollars a year. The urgent care services in the building had closed a couple of years prior to 2008. In short, it was called a "brown field" in Lean terms.

On the other hand, the physicians and staff were very aware of the problems facing the clinic and had been trying ways to improve for a number of years. They had lobbied unsuccessfully for what they perceived as needed additional resources for several years. They were desperate for improvement in the work environment, and some entertained thoughts of moving on if the situation did not improve. When Lean was offered as a potential solution, there was a good deal of skepticism, but that was overcome by their desperation to get better. So, they accepted the challenge.

Since Lean started at the clinic, there has been only a minimum of additional system resources added in the form of money for remodeling some modular furniture and walls, and changes in signage. The system did fund a Lean team and consultant for 3 months. The clinic's success story was created largely on the basis of their own internal resources and people.

Although I have personally declared them a success story, the purpose of this chapter is not only to share their success but also to lead readers to ponder their own view of what success looks like. Some, after reading the chapter, might not be willing to declare a success. That could be because they do not feel like adequate results were obtained. Or it could be because they are reluctant to ever declare success in a Lean transformation, as it is a continuous improvement journey with no ending point. I would prefer to celebrate stages of success while recognizing that, even when the celebration occurs, there are ongoing efforts to continue to improve.

This story is also meant to raise the challenge that success might look different over time and at different stages of a Lean transformation. I would encourage the reader to follow the chapter sequentially and not look to the end to see what happened some 15 months after the completion of the Lean implementation phase. That would be somewhat like reading the last chapter of a mystery book before reading the rest. Some of the joy is in the discoveries made during the journey.

In January 2008, the newly formed Lean team and a Lean consultant arrived at the clinic. They spent the next 100 days or so full time at the clinic. With the exception of the consultant, they were inexperienced and were nervous and wondering how they could possibly perform any of their other duties that were temporarily set aside and still get this work done. The staff at the clinic was perhaps more nervous, and rumors had already started to circulate that Lean was just a plot to get rid of employees. Through group meetings and one-on-one dialogues, trust and confidence began to emerge.

A team of staff members was empowered to rearrange and redesign the clinic break room as an introduction to 6S. They completely rearranged the room, got rid of old, battered, and largely unused lockers, repainted, and did 6S. They were very proud of the break room they created over the next 2 weeks. They could easily find what they needed and clearly recognized the value of 6S. About the same time, one of the supervisors got so excited about single piece flow that she made changes in medical records previously described in Chapter 1. There were several positive results, but one of the most striking had to do with keeping current with loose filing. Clinics all over the system had unsuccessfully tried different methods to keep current with loose filing. But single piece flow worked, and there was visual "before and after" evidence (see Figure 10.1).

The news about the success with the loose filing spread rapidly around the organization. Other local successes included:

- 60% reduction in cycle times for patient visits.
- The percentage of telephone calls answered within 1 min went from 40% to 80%–100%.
- Requests for prescription refills were filled the same day.
- Physicians began getting all their work done at the office and leaving for home earlier and earlier.
- 270 improvement ideas were identified in the project priority matrix. They ranged from simple steps of moving equipment closer to the work to complex process redesign.

Pictures of the loose filing and other successes were shared with many people in the organization, including senior leaders and the quality committee of the board. Staff and physicians at the site were excited about the outcomes they were achieving. Everyone was optimistic about results that would follow. After the implementation phase (April 2008), one member of the system Lean team stayed behind but the rest moved on to another site, and the local clinic improvement teams set about working on the long list of improvement ideas.

Three months after the completion of the implementation phase, site performance profiles began to emerge. The report (now 6 months since the start of the effort) contained revenue, cost, patient satisfaction, and turnover measures (see Figure 10.2a–c). There was no change in revenue, cost, or patient satisfaction. There was a drop in employee turnover that was not statistically significant. At this point, how would someone view the information in terms of success? There are some positive changes that occurred but no impact to the bottom line. Should someone expect to see impact on financials at this point? In the actual circumstance, the reaction was generally that there seemed to be some promising early outcomes, but people would take a "wait-and-see" attitude. In the meantime, there was no real incremental cost, and the physicians and staff in the clinic were continuing to work on the items on the project priority matrix.

More Batching

Example:

16 inches of loose filing waiting to go in charts:

• Progress notes

• Consults

• Test results

• Messages

Improving the health of individuals, families and communities 🏛 **PRESBYTERIAN**

Filing Done Just in Time

Example:

Continuous flow delivery of medical records actually created more time for just in time filing.

Result: Zero inches of loose filing

Improving the health of individuals, families and communities 🏛 **PRESBYTERIAN**

Figure 10.1   Loose filing before and after single piece flow.

Although people were reviewing reports on a monthly basis, at the end of the fiscal year (now 10 months since the completion of the implementation phase) a new profile of progress was completed.

There were several promising findings. Compared to the prior year:

▪ Net revenue increased $182,480.
▪ The cost of labor hours decreased by $243,750, which was the equivalent of 6.5 FTEs.
▪ Overtime costs decreased $52,515.

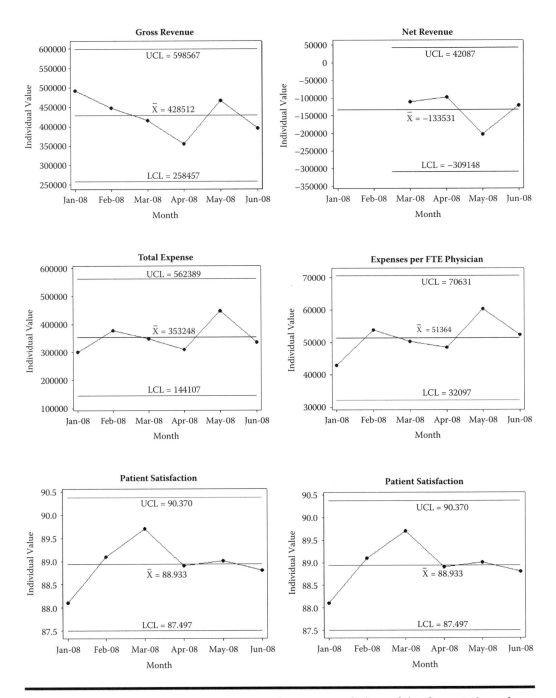

Figure 10.2 (a) Gross/net revenue—3 months postcompletion of implementation phase; (b) Expense and expense per FTE physician—3 months postcompletion of implementation phase. (c) Patient satisfaction and employee turnover—3 months postcompletion of implementation phase.

- Supply costs decreased $21,782.
- Internal medicine physicians added a total of 46 appointment slots per week to the scheduling template.
- There was a clear decrease in employee turnover overall, and it became more stable with less variation from month to month.
- 243 of 270 of improvement projects initially identified (as well as other projects) were completed.

However, there was no change in the overall financial picture or patient satisfaction (see Figure 10.3a–c). How would someone view the year-to-year reduction in labor hours and supply costs? Should someone write it off to variation or view it as promising early results? If 100% of the improvement projects were completed, why was there still no obvious impact to the bottom line?

Would someone view more phone calls answered within a minute and the subsequent decrease in disconnects as only a patient satisfaction indicator? Could it be a precursor for a subsequent reduction in labor costs? Answering phones promptly could lead to a reduction in callback labor. Should the fact that the internists voluntarily added 46 total appointment slots among them be viewed as a precursor to increased gross revenue? Or would cost and revenue stay proportionately the same resulting in no net gain in revenue? Should it be attributed to a recent organizational effort to increase physician productivity to the 50th (and subsequently 60th) percentile or to increased capacity and efficiency from the Lean effort? These questions and others like them are not always easy to answer.

While the people in finance and other senior leaders were encouraging, they were not willing to recognize any credit toward a return on investment (ROI). There was growing organizational emphasis that the Lean efforts needed to result in a positive ROI.

The work on improvement projects in the clinic continued. In early 2009, some encouraging signs began to appear in the clinic profile. For 4 out of 5 months, gross revenue was higher than the previous 12 month average. In April, for the first time ever the clinic had positive net revenue ($46,778) (Figure 10.4a). In addition, there was less month-to-month variation in total expense (Figure 10.4b). There was some improvement in patient satisfaction, but it was not statistically significant (Figure 10.4d). There was some increase in employee turnover coincident with a major change in management throughout the medical group (Figure 10.4c) that involved replacing administrative managers with clinical nurse managers. In addition, the duties of clerical supervisors were assumed by the clinical nurse supervisors. There was significant turmoil associated with the changes.

The finance people were still not convinced these were real trends that would last and result in hard dollar savings; however, people became increasingly interested in seeing the monthly reports. The improved outcome trends continued all the way up to the end-of-the-year reports (Figure 10.5a–g).

The trend of increased gross revenue continued throughout 2009. When comparing 2008 and 2009, there was an 11% increase ($5,640,410) in gross revenue (Table 10.1/Figure 10.5a). The RVU production per FTE physician is characterized by very large increases in 4 months of 2009, with the remainder of months in 2009 unchanged or less than 2008. There was an unusually bad influenza season in the fall/winter of 2009/2010, which may have contributed to some of the increased productivity; however, the additional appointment capacity added by physicians earlier in the transformation effort would certainly be a contributor. What should someone conclude from these control charts? Is there a real and sustainable improvement?

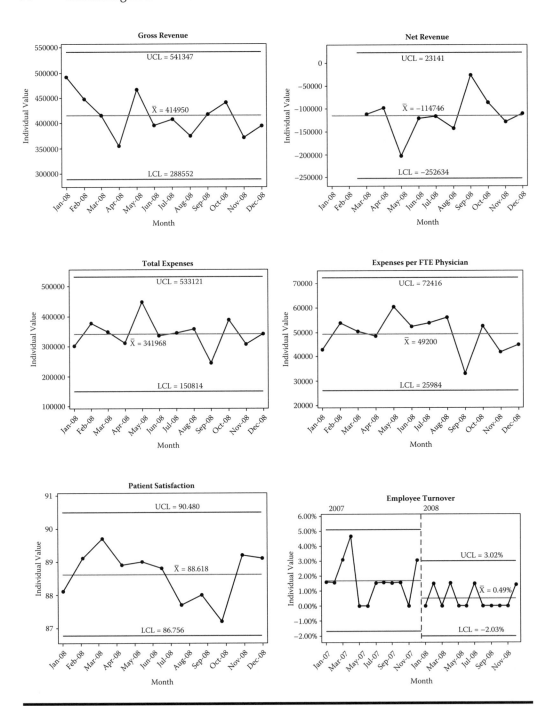

Figure 10.3 (a) Gross and net revenue—9 months postcompletion of implementation phase; (b) Total expense and expense per FTE physician—9 months postcompletion of implementation phase; (c) Patient satisfaction and employee turnover—9 months postcompletion of implementation phase.

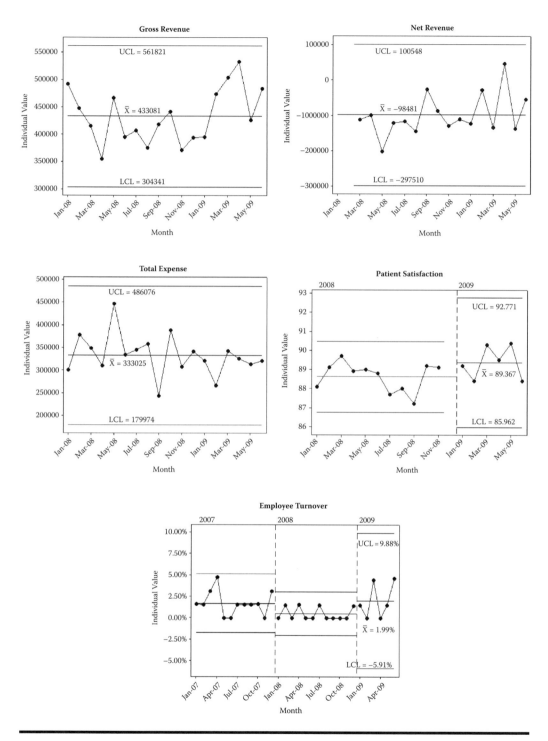

Figure 10.4   (a) Gross and net revenue—15 months postcompletion of implementation phase; (b) Total expense—15 months postcompletion of implementation phase; (c) Patient satisfaction—15 months postcompletion of implementation phase; (d) Employee turnover—15 months postcompletion of implementation phase.

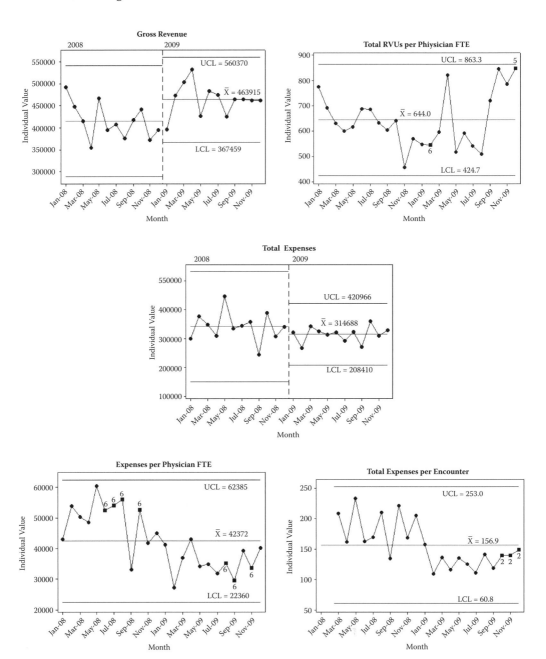

Figure 10.5 **(a)** Gross revenue and RVUs per physician—21 months postimplementation phase; **(b)** Total expenses—21 months postimplementation phase; **(c)** Expense per physician FTE and encounter—21 months postimplementation phase; **(d)** Salary and supply expense per FTE physician—21 months postimplementation phase; **(e)** Net revenue and net revenue per physician FTE—21 months postimplementation phase; **(f)** Employee turnover—21 months postimplementation phase; **(g)** Patient satisfaction—21 months postimplementation phase.

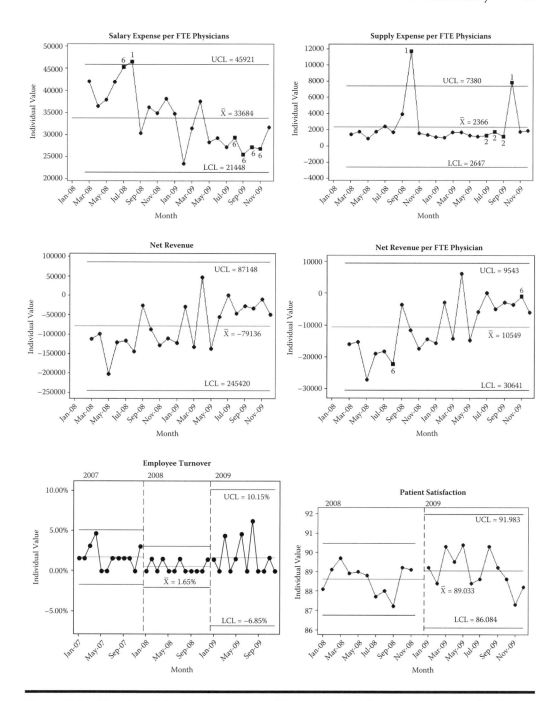

Figure 10.5 (Continued) (a) Gross revenue and RVUs per physician—21 months postimplementation phase; (b) Total expenses—21 months postimplementation phase; (c) Expense per physician FTE and encounter—21 months postimplementation phase; (d) Salary and supply expense per FTE physician—21 months postimplementation phase; (e) Net revenue and net revenue per physician FTE—21 months postimplementation phase; (f) Employee turnover—21 months postimplementation phase; (g) Patient satisfaction—21 months postimplementation phase.

Table 10.1   Financial Gains in the Second Year of the Lean Effort

	2008	*2009*		
Category	*Total*	*Total*	*Net Change*	*% Change*
Gross patient revenue	$41,071,031,010	$5,543,448	$5,640,410	11%
Total expenses	$4,103,612	$37,762,510	$327,353	8%
Salary expenses	$26,105,086	$2,614,232	$80,854	3%
Supply expenses[a]	$202,332	$1,103,817	$8,515	4%
Net revenue	$1,147,464	$4,421,048	$704,516	310%

[a] There was an additional $21,782 decrease in supply costs in 2008 compared to 2007.

There was a decrease in total expenses of about 8% (–$327,353) (Table 10.1/Figure 10.5b), which was not statistically significant; however, when one looks at the total expenses per FTE physician and per encounter (Figure 10.5c), there was an impressive and statistically significant decrease in expenses. The patient care process in the clinic had become much more efficient. The decreased cycle time for patient encounters, prescription refills, and patient callbacks experienced earlier in the transformation appears to have been early process improvement indicators for the reductions in expense incurred at these later dates.

The salary expenses per FTE physician began trending downward, beginning in late summer 2008 and reached statistical significance in the late summer of 2009 (Figure 10.5d). They decreased 3% (–$80,854) compared to 2008 (Table 10.1). There were additional savings of $121,870 for professional fees in 2008 that were no longer necessary in 2009. Here again, there were early indicators that more salary savings would occur later in the process. The reduction in labor hours that occurred in 2008 was indeed a harbinger of future savings; however, at that point, there was only the year-to-year comparison between 2007 and 2008. Now there was trended data to confirm the savings over a longer period of time.

At the beginning of the implementation phase in January 2008, while doing 6S, there was more than $10,000 worth of expired supplies that were discovered and had to be discarded. The installed Kanban system is designed to reliably decrease costs immediately, and one would expect those savings to continue indefinitely. Supply costs for 2009 were decreased 4% ($8,515) (Table 10.1). The supply costs in 2008 were already decreased compared to 2007 ($21,782), so there was a collective savings of $302,107 for the 2 years compared to 2007. Savings began immediately once 6S was applied to supply rooms, and Kanban started in January 2008. The two statistically significant peaks in supply costs in October of each year were for the purchase of influenza vaccine (Figure 10.5d).

Net revenue continued with a trended increase throughout 2009, resulting in a statistically significant increase in net revenue per physician (Figure 10.5e). There was a 310% ($704,516) increase in net revenue when compared to 2008. Each physician became more productive as the impact of the Lean improvement projects broadened. They were paid on a productivity basis, and there was a continued organizational push to increase productivity. Where should the credit be given? Perhaps credit should be given to both factors; however, one must remember that the physicians were achieving these increases and still going home each day earlier than when they were less productive in 2008. Improved productivity and less time spent in the office could not have occurred without the Lean effort.

The decreased employee turnover that occurred in 2008 and the first 2 months of 2009 was impressive. The subsequent increase in turnover that occurred at least coincident in time with the changes in management is just a reminder that having a Lean working environment does not prevent employee turnover if other factors are at play in the workplace. Employee turnover did return to the 2008 baseline in the last quarter of 2009. It is not known if that low level of turnover continued.

Perhaps the most disappointing outcome is the lack of change in patient satisfaction. As I indicated earlier, Lean is not primarily a patient satisfaction improvement methodology; however, Lean is really driven from the patient's view of the world. That, combined with faster cycle times and improved response times, might be expected to impact patient satisfaction scores. In this case, scores did not improve. The reasons are unknown.

I would be remiss if I did not mention that the clinic already had strong performance in quality outcomes, including national benchmark performance in glucose control among diabetics. The high standards of clinical performance continued throughout the Lean transformation.

The financial improvement is difficult to refute. Although there are always going to be background factors such as seasonal variation in infectious disease, organizational efforts to improve productivity, or reduce the workforce (what I collectively term "background noise") that impact findings, the trend lines in this case are steady. None of the other primary care clinics experienced this dramatic improvement in financial performance during this time, even though the factors referred to earlier were impacting all of them. The other clinics either had not started Lean or were in the early stages before one would expect to see similar improvements.

I hope the learnings from this chapter will help the reader gain a time-based focus on judging success. Early in the transformation, there will most likely only be process improvement indicators and short-term labor savings. They should be viewed as early indicators that the sustained improvements in hard dollars should come no later than 12–20 months in the future. It is during that time that the important work of implementing all the improvement ideas is occurring. The lag in financial performance improvement is, I believe, because of all the improvement work that needs completion. The financial results will follow. For that to happen, the staff, physicians, and senior leaders will need to work hard to sustain the gains and continue to improve during the critical months following the implementation phase.

Chapter 11

Sustaining

When the organizational Lean team has departed the site, the role of the physician, manager and supervisor and members of the site Lean team becomes most important. It has been my premise throughout the book that physicians, who stand to gain the most benefit through improvements in operational efficiency, should have a role in being accountable for sustained success. For far too long, healthcare organizations, particularly in large integrated systems, have been focused on "getting physicians to do what they do best and that is see patients." While I agree with that premise, there also needs to be some time for them to observe and make suggestions for improvement about the work environment in addition to working on teams to actually implement the improvements. Physicians at times tend to be autocratic and very directive to others in terms of what they want. Beyond that façade, I believe that physicians have inherent thinking skills, founded on repetitive use of the scientific method in clinical decision making, to be key supporters for improvement efforts.

Physicians, along with other clinicians such as nursing staff, spend more time at the *gemba* than anyone else. Their work productivity and satisfaction is dependent on an efficient workplace. As such, they should take advantage of this and watch for improvement opportunities. They should join other leaders on gemba walks or at a minimum meet with managers and supervisors regularly about the results of standard work, assessments, visual controls, etc. They should take care to note observations on improvement boards or huddle boards and share them with staff, improvement teams, and managers. Physicians may have stopped doing this some time ago because of a perceived lack of responsiveness from management, but now would be the time to reinvest in the improvement process and become an active participant.

Physicians may also be reluctant to point out the mistakes of their peers or lack of adoption of Lean tools and standard work by their peers.

> Doctors are deeply reluctant to point out the mistakes of others, much less officially reprimand one another, knowing that they all hide mistakes and being sympathetic to the pressures faced by colleagues.[1]
>
> **John Troussaint, MD**

In a Lean environment, it is vital for physicians to hold one another accountable for accepting and executing standards developed by the group. Examples include standard exam rooms, patient preps, test results notification, etc. The reason is simple: nonstandard care processes consume resources and waste the time and energy of staff, as well as create greater risk of error. The example earlier in the book of temporary or PRN employees taking more than twice as long to accomplish routine tasks compared to full-time employees before standard work was developed reflects that difference. Variations in the care process between physicians and lack of adoption of Lean principles and tools should be viewed as opportunities for learning and improvement. The reasons for variation and lack of adoption should be explored with peers and, if applicable, used as an opportunity to improve processes and use of Lean tools.

The days of just verbally expressing a concern or issue and simply expecting someone to solve the problem should be long gone by the time a site enters the sustain phase. In a Lean environment, every problem identified and every improvement suggestion made should go into a reliable process for assessment, followed by PDSA attempts to make improvements. Physicians have the responsibility to put the message about the issue properly in the new process.

After the core Lean team leaves the site, there will be three to five staff members who served on the Lean implementation team who are now returning to their previous jobs full time. They have a key role to fulfill during the sustain phase. They are now among the most knowledgeable staff regarding Lean approaches, tools, and principles. They should be members of the site Lean team and be given time to lead improvement teams and teach others, particularly new employees. They become the keepers of the site collective knowledge. The site Lean team will now function much as the organization core team did during the implementation phase. Once the implementation is done, some of them will want to go on and serve as Lean specialists for the organization. In one of our clinics, all of the site Lean team members were allowed to go on and assume new roles as Lean specialists in other locations. However, it was a mistake because the clinic was then left with a minimum of Lean knowledge and experience needed for sustaining the gains. As the number of sites grew, more Lean specialists were needed in other parts of the organization, but we always kept in mind the needs of the site left behind and left adequate resources to be able to sustain.

Lean Work

While the emphasis will be greater on the improvement model and repetitive PDCA cycles during the sustain phase, sites will need to maintain proficiency of Lean tools and principles.

Kanban will need to be applied to new products that will be used in the patient care process, including use of calculations to establish par values and creation of new Kanban cards. 6S will need constant assessment because of the tendency to backslide and create clutter in the work area. As work processes are changed, new labor analysis may be needed. For instance, if a new lab or image ordering process is planned, or a new registration process is developed, a new labor analysis may be needed to determine the number of FTEs required to do the new work. It is possible for the new process to require fewer FTEs or, conversely, more people if the process outcomes are improved quality, safety, or cycle times for patients.

Single piece flow involves continuous work to remove unnecessary steps. Our tendency to revert to batching is very strong and needs constant attention. I recently experienced what may be the ultimate practical experience I have had involving single piece flow. I stayed in a very large hotel that probably holds thousands of guests. The elevators for the entire hotel were centrally

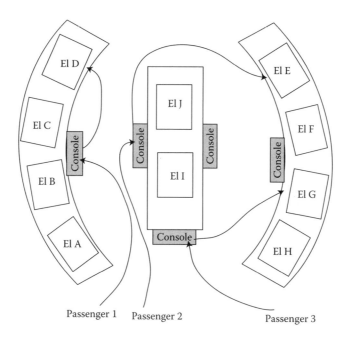

Figure 11.1 Elevator process using single piece flow.

located around a column of two elevators. I expected to experience the usual rush of people during breaks or at the end of meetings, all trying to grab an elevator and, when they missed, trying to guess which elevator would be next and positioning themselves next to it. Imagine my surprise when I never saw more than two or three people waiting for an elevator and I never rode with more than three others. And no, the hotel was not deserted!

Their system treated each guest as someone with an individual need. The guest would go to a console located around the bank of elevators and punch in their desired floor. There were several consoles to choose from. The console would then display directions for which elevator to go to based on expected arrival time (see Figure 11.1). I never waited more than seconds and frequently rode by myself. Even in this circumstance where, as a customer, I was blown away, I was told that they were working on making it even better. It will be vital for sites to retain staff that are fully trained and knowledgeable regarding Lean tools and principles, as well as be well versed in the improvement model.

Improvement Work

> A lean healthcare organization trains people in problem-solving, then respects their opinions and experience enough to let them take the lead on improvement.[1]
>
> **John Toussaint, MD**

It will be critical for managers, supervisors, physicians, and site-based Lean specialists to trust the frontline staff to do the improvement work. They will need leadership, but it should be by stewardship rather than autocratic controlling styles.

Table 11.1 Potential Daily/Weekly Healthcare Monitoring Measures

Patient cycle times: ED, clinic, hospital, lab, imaging, etc.	Percentage of patients with ventilator-associated pneumonia bundles: ICU
Cycle times for prescription refills and messages returned: primarily clinics	Percentage of patients with central line insertion bundle: hospital
Lab turnaround times: ED, hospital, clinics	Percentage of on time starts: OR
Number of patients seen per hour: ED, clinics	Turnaround times: OR
Number of patients who left without being seen: ED	Imaging turnaround times: ED, clinic, hospital
Wait times for inpatient bed: ED, PACU, clinics	Number of patient falls: long-term care, SNF, hospital
Door to balloon time: ED	Percentage of patients with postdischarge calls: Ed, hospital, clinics
Phones answered in seconds/minutes: ED, clinics, call centers, etc.	Percentage of patients prepared for surgery correctly: OR

> Stewardship is defined as the willingness to be accountable for the well being of the larger organization by operating in service, rather than in control, of those around us.[2]

Leadership characterized by stewardship is also known as "servant leadership."

> The first order of business is to build a group of people who, under the influence of the institution, grow taller and become healthier, stronger, and more autonomous.[3]

Frontline staff should be empowered to create improvement ideas and test them for virtually any work process; however, servant leadership does not equate with empowering the staff without accountability for financial and quality consequences. It does equate to leaders providing the vision and strategy as an organization to use as a reference for improvement ideas. Using the improvement model, ideas should be tested and measured for effectiveness before any decision to implement the idea on a departmental or systemwide basis.

Not everyone selected to be members of a Lean site team during implementation will work out to be good leaders. Those who find it difficult to deal with resistance or having a persuasive influence on others will have difficulty functioning in the role as a leader once the sustain phase is in place. They should be mentored and developed to be more comfortable with change management. They may also be good team members providing technical assistance to improvement teams without having to serve as team leaders.

Empowering staff to be responsible for solving problems and developing improvement ideas is not synonymous with their being responsible for identifying all problems and improvement ideas. In actuality, it is managers and supervisors who typically identify improvement opportunities. Managers and supervisors are ultimately responsible for supporting the improvement process and making sure that improvement teams are constantly working on newly identified problems.

There should be a site Lean team in each site that functions in perpetuity. Members of the team will likely consist of those who participated in the implementation phase, as well as others who have shown promise and skills for Lean and improvement work. The team would have responsibility for managing the improvement board (moving identified problems, to "being worked on" "in testing," "sustaining," etc.). Daily huddles should occur around the improvement board, and the team should be meeting weekly with administrative and physician leaders to review progress.

Someone from the Lean team should have responsibility for venue (potentially at staff meetings, providers meetings, or separate meetings) for sharing successes and challenges created from the improvement work at the site. They do not, however, have to present the materials. Recruiting other staff who have worked on a particular improvement project will help mentor and develop Lean skills and confidence in others.

Monitoring

In addition, physicians and staff should be provided data on a daily or weekly basis regarding process outcomes trended overtime. Graphed data should be presented on core care processes, as well as any process where there is an improvement effort underway. Examples could include:

It is important to note that these are just examples. Many others may be appropriate in different settings. Also important to note is that many of these measures are routinely reported on a monthly basis in system reports. However, a monthly reporting frequency is not conducive to supporting improvement work. Real time (or as close to real time as possible), which means daily or weekly reporting, is required in a Lean environment for improvement work to progress. In addition, the results should be posted in a clearly visible space where physicians and staff have ready access. These could be great examples of visual controls.

I am aware of one ED that posted an ED board. It contained various process elements from the previous day. A report was produced electronically and posted for the previous day's results. Measures included, among others: (1) time of day triage had to be started, (2) ED to bed times, (3) lab, imaging, and transport turnaround times, (4) patient arrival to bed time, (5) time from patient put in bed until physician attends, etc. They have a huddle twice a day to review the previous day's results and set goals for the current day. Having the more immediate feedback has proven vital for them to improve their patient care process.

Written standard work for physicians around monitoring current conditions should exist and at a minimum include:

- Participation in daily huddles
- Daily review of visual controls
- Timely review of other reports relating to the efficiency and efficacy of the patient care process at their location

Written standard work for lead physicians should also include:

- Regular participation in scheduled department/clinic Lean team meetings
- Weekly, if not daily, check in with a manager or supervisor regarding rounding or assessments
- Weekly gemba walk

Time needed to perform this standard work for frontline physicians should take no more than 10–15 min. The standard work for physician leaders no more than 90 min a week. If those items are in place and process outcome data shows improvement, there is an excellent chance for a successful transition from implementation to long-term sustainment.

Communications

Communication during the sustain phase is as important, if not more so, than during the implementation phase. Typically, additional communication channels are opened up during an implementation phase and might include newsletters devoted only to Lean, special meetings devoted only to Lean, new bulletin boards, etc. It is not uncommon for people to perceive those efforts as temporary additional work that can be abandoned once the implementation phase is over, and the core Lean team has left the site. On the contrary, the communication plan during the sustain phase has an important role.

If those additional communication channels are abandoned, it is an indirect message that the site staff can now go back to their old ways of working. The Lean communications need to stay active and are a way of letting people know how they work is going to remain changed to the current state and not regress to old work habits. The exact methods don't have to stay the same, but there should be continued specific focus on Lean. Continued focus on Lean and the improvement work of people and teams at the site is an important factor in continued success.

I had a follow-up conversation with a physician several months after a Lean implementation in a clinic. I knew that a great deal of the Lean culture has persisted, as well as use of tools and practices. However, when I spoke about how successful they had been, he responded that he didn't see any sign of Lean still being around. He could not see the culture change and different work methodologies in spite of the fact his own staff had standard work and were using the tools. Without the reinforcement that the improvements really are about Lean and improvement work, the tendency to drift back to old work patterns will be strong.

Storytelling is a powerful way to keep the Lean culture sustained. Giving staff and others throughout the organization time to come together to share their success stories is uplifting and motivating. Thedacare has a weekly session in an auditorium that is usually packed where different improvement teams come together to share their success stories. It not only motivates others when they see someone being successful, it is a powerful idea propagator for spread of new and innovative ideas.

A communication plan should also include a mechanism to report progress to senior leaders and others in the organization. The message needs to be succinct and to the point. One method used very successfully is called a 5-UP report (see Table 11.2). Leaders found it very helpful, quick, and easy to assimilate. Use of the 5-UP is also quite useful during the implementation phase.

The other factor to keep in mind when developing and implementing a communication plan for the sustain phase is that repetition is essential. One only has to think about communication with patients and how frequently they leave our offices either totally confused or uncertain about follow-up plans and medication usage. They often don't have an idea why a particular medication was prescribed or even why they are going to see someone on consultation.

In addition, there will be some staff turnover. Hopefully, it will be less than when Lean was started. However, communication needs to be repetitive because every year there will be a new group of people who haven't heard the message. Typically, organizations turn to training programs to bring new staff up to speed on a particular topic. Ironically, it is not uncommon to have the training look nothing like what is going on at a particular site. Keeping the Lean culture alive

Table 11.2   5-UP Report

Site Lean Implementation 5-UP Report	
Current Week Activity	**Next Week Planned Activities**
• Huddle standard work developed with the managers • Core team in CAP training for 3 days • Kanban cards with water spider in pod B • Standardization of rooms in progress • Provider meetings for fast orders to be done • Established with manager the huddle, assessment, and attendance tracking tools • Project board and metrics relocated into hall • Review of deliverable items and deadlines	• Standard work for clinical and other areas • Tool training and documentations for sustain • Cross-training matrix for all departments • Assessments for huddles • Kanban process for supplies in • Transition plan reviewed at the Wed all-staff meeting • Go forward plan roughed out' • Sustain plan roughed out • Duplicate med record root cause analysis • Prioritization matrix updated • Capture quotes for accomplishments
Key Metrics/Key Observations	**Lessons Learned**
• Wed all-staff team meeting went well related to structure, topics, attitudes • Huddles have large variation in content and process • Inconsistent process to work project board	• Visual cues implemented in the process as soon as appropriate—huddle boards, project boards, assessment sheets
Obstacles	
• No engagement of frontline staff and no plan in place to recruit as team leads on projects • Too many conflicting priorities with multiple initiative roll-outs (PCSC, med reconciliation, progress notes, fast orders)	

through communication and constantly teaching tools and techniques at the site needs to be an integral part of new employee on-boarding.

Finally, there is the question of how much is enough. Probably, everyone has heard the concept that it takes a minimum of eight exposures to a new idea for a person to grasp the concept. Eight repetitions of the Lean message are probably not enough because not everyone will hear or see the message every time. The communication methods used should be varied and frequent. It is probably not possible to overcommunicate the messages.

Standardization

Once implementation is complete and the sustain phase well in place, it is, unfortunately, easy for people to slip back into old habits when making changes. A little change here, a little there, adds up to creating a lot of variation. The healthcare worker inclination to fix things reveals itself when something goes wrong, and a solution can be implemented quickly to fix the problem. The result is eventually what we started with before Lean was implemented and overly complex processes that function poorly.

To not only maintain but improve three things must be in place. 1) Any changes made must be vetted through the PDSA cycle and, if approved, spread to everyone else affected by the process change. (2) When dealing with different pods (clinical work areas in the same general location), nursing units, multiple clinics, hospitals, etc., there must be a mechanism in place to ensure that any changes are reviewed organizationally and, if approved, deployed across all areas. (3) Standard work for leaders (including physician leaders) must be in place, and accountable individuals need to be executing the standard work.

Any changes or suggestions for changes should be captured on the improvement board and go through the PDSA cycle. That does not mean it has to be a long-drawn-out process. Someone with a simple suggestion can post the problem or improvement idea, and go through small tests of change. Not all things will require the work of an entire Lean team, but ideas must be tested and measured with the results reviewed and acted on by the Lean team. One would hope that the resources at a site would be sufficient, so that many tests of change can be occurring at the same time. Many improvement teams may be working at the same time in different areas with subsequent outcomes of their work reviewed by the site Lean team. While the site Lean team may be working on their own improvement project, they have an equally, if not more, important role in reviewing results for potential deployment recommendations across departments or organizations.

If the sustain phase is going well, there will be many improvement projects occurring at any given point in time. Some people at different sites may be working on the same process and not even know about the others' work. Without a central clearing house to coordinate the improvement suggestions, variation and nonstandard work processes will result. One might think of it as a macro PDSA cycle (see Figure 11.2).

This approach is modeled after the Toyota model for maintaining standardization. The clerical and clinical teams should be composed of frontline staff from different departments and locations within an organization. While they may have a manager or leader as part of the team, the function of the team should not be executed by a group of managers or supervisors. The acceptance or rejection of an improvement idea should be made by frontline staffs who work with the process on a regular basis. Improvement ideas that have been tested and found to be an effective improvement would be sent along with any pertinent measurement data to the clinical or clerical team for review, and recommendation regarding deployment throughout the appropriate departments or sites in the organization. These teams would be permanent with perhaps rotating term limits for members of the team to add fresh perspective over time.

Once a recommendation for deployment is made, it should not be mandated across all locations. The recommendation for deploying the new process should include an invitation for different sites to do their own testing on the suggestion before fully implementing. During the testing, new sites may discover further improvements or discover that in their circumstance the new process would need modification. This would then create another macro PDSA cycle with resubmission of the variation or improvement idea to the central team for further review. The standardization process executed in this manner creates a culture of continuous improvement.

Standard work for leaders will have some variation from site to site and leader to leader, depending on the nature of the work and the role of the leader. However, standard work for leaders in

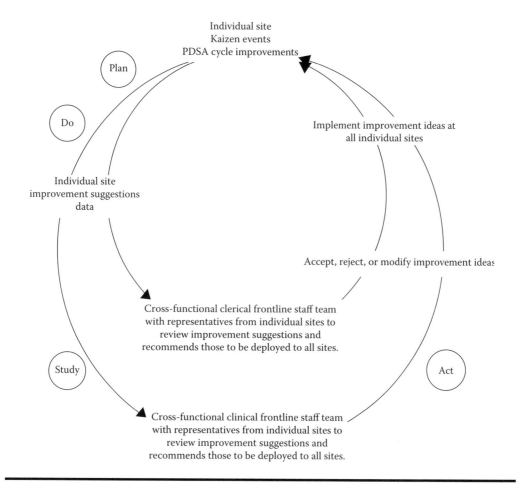

Figure 11.2 Standardization during sustain phase.

the same category (e.g., leads, supervisors, managers, physicians, etc.) should have common core elements. These include:

- Gemba walks
- Performing assessments
- Monitoring process outcomes and results
- Participation on Lean site teams
- Ensuring visual controls are maintained
- Ensuring a Lean culture is maintained

In addition to standard work for leaders, standard work for staff should be in place. Coincident with that effort, human resource departments should be working with other departments to standardize and simplify job descriptions. Typically, in a successful Lean transformation, the number and complexity of job descriptions decrease dramatically in an effort to mirror standard work. Lean also requires individuals to be able to work in different staff roles that simplified job descriptions help to support.

Summary

In summary, the key elements that need to be in place for success during the sustain phase include:

- Leader (including physicians) standard work
- Accountability from leaders to execute the standard work on a daily basis
- Visual controls
- Adherence to the improvement model throughout the organization
- Robust measurement systems that create data and information
- Servant leadership leading to staff empowerment to solve problems
- Daily huddles

While there are many other factors that contribute to success, without these key core elements in place, achieving a sustainable Lean transformation will be difficult at best. Conversely, executing on these elements, even without all the other potential factors, will help ensure long-term success.

References

1. John Toussaint, Roger A. Gerard, and Emily Adams. *On the Mend: Revolutionizing Health Care to Save Lives and Transform the Industry.* Cambridge: Lean Enterprise Institute, Inc., 2010.
2. Peter Block. *Stewardship: Choosing Service over Self Interest.* San Francisco: Berrett-Koehler, 1993.
3. Robert K. Greenleaf. *Servant Leadership A Journey into the Nature of Legitimate Power and Greatness.* Paulist Press, New York, 1997.

Chapter 12

PreImplementation Tools and Approaches

What follows are some tools and approaches that can be used when preparing to begin a Lean implementation at any location.

Site Lean Team Selection: Roles and Responsibilities

The Site Team

The team should include 4–6 people, depending on the size of the site. Membership should come primarily from frontline staff, but management may be included. Members need to be supportive of the Lean process for the achievement of the PHS vision, mission, and goals. Members should be at ease talking with and influencing peers, management, etc., and able to effectively respond to challenges.

Purpose of Site Team

While the team will have many responsibilities, their primary purpose can be summarized in a few key points:

- To analyze current state and use data to work with other frontline staff and management on design and implementation of process excellence improvements
- To be a primary resource in implementing improvements
- To act as a group of individuals that have been thoroughly trained in continuous improvement principles and techniques
- To provide leadership, knowledge, mentoring, and training to the site

Characteristics of Site Team Leaders and Members

The team you select will have considerable responsibility. They will be setting the expectations and directing the momentum of the site as it relates to how business will be conducted in the future. Some characteristics include:

- *Attitude*: Unquenchable drive to improve processes: curious, imaginative, and insightful
- *Leadership*: "Soft skills"; respect of others within the organization; ability to create, facilitate, train, and lead teams to success; confident and respected across the site
- *Change agent*: Ability to manage projects, reach closure, and drive to timely completion of projects
- *Communication*: Ability to communicate with strong interpersonal and presentation skills
- *Basic analytical skills*: Ability to learn, apply, and wisely link tools, some of which may utilize computer applications, common sense, and logical reasoning

This list does not call for a strong knowledge of statistical techniques or Lean fundamentals. Individuals with the characteristics listed earlier will pick up these technical elements, if provided with good instructional material and training. The "soft skills" are as important, if not more important, than "hard skills."

Soft skills that all team members should possess include:

- Balanced concern for people and business issues
- Unquestioned integrity
- Willingness to take personal and professional risks
- Willingness to challenge traditions and ask the hard or unpopular questions ("why")
- Ability to be an effective facilitator
- Ability to speak candidly with and effectively influence senior management and front-line employees
- Ability to disassociate from bias and challenge the status quo
- Ability to diplomatically handle complex situations and complex personalities
- Ability to conduct constructive and critical personal evaluation and admit error
- Ability to manage conflict and persevere through the challenges that come with change
- Ability to be self-aware of being effective
- Self-starter and able to proactively address issues and risks as they surface, or are recognized
- Resilience
- Ability to communicate with docs and upper management

Identifying Site Team Leaders

You should choose 4–6 team members, depending on the size of the site and the scope of the project. The team composition should be a mixture of frontline staff and leadership. A diverse group is encouraged, as it will help to spread this initiative throughout the healthcare system, as well as provide different points of view.

Frontline staff are expected to be full time and must have duties transferred to PRN or other employees. Managers or supervisors may be team members and are expected to participate 80% of the time. Every attempt will be made to backfill their positions. A supervisor or manager may or may not be chosen as the team leader and must be able to set aside their authority and participate within the team as an equal.

Prior to the selection process potential candidates must know the requirements to be a team member:

- The team will be dedicated to the Lean project full time. Typical project length is 12 weeks.
- Hours per day will vary depending on the activities being performed. There may be 10–12 hour days during the project.
- Team members must have computer skills and be proficient in the use of Microsoft Excel, PowerPoint, and Word. Most of the project will be done using Excel, and it is imperative that all team members know and feel comfortable with Excel.
- Team members will play a vital role in change management. They must be at ease when talking to their peers, management, and other team members in order to drive change and influence and respond to challenges from each of these groups. Team members must be able to manage conflicting opinions without judgment.

PreImplementation Checklist

	Item	*Notes*
1	Complete preimplementation assessment	
2	A change management plan is in place	
3	Meetings with providers held by champions and organization physician leader for Lean	
4	Initiate project charter	
5	Identify contacts for each support service department	
6	HR department has been contacted	
7	Team members are aware of and committed to project start/completion timeline and working hours	
8	4–6 team members have been selected and committed to the project for the full duration	
9	Lean team space identified for duration of implementation	
10	Implementation visioning—kick-off meeting scheduled	
11	Stakeholder analysis meeting scheduled	
12	Training plan initiated	
13	2–h Lean overview sessions with frontline employees have been scheduled	
14	Frontline management expectations, roles, and responsibilities meeting (1 h) has been scheduled	
15	Present deployment timeline	

(Continued)

(Continued)

	Item	*Notes*
16	The department staff has received verbal communication regarding the project	
17	Backfill in place as needed	
18	Materials and supplies ordered	
19	All tools and supplies are available for the team	
20	One computer per team member with required software and access is available on project start date	
21	A "hold" area with tables or shelves is available	
22	Rollout workforce Lean culture survey	
23	Establish communication plan (newsletters, team meetings, huddles, communication boards)	
24	Obtain floor plans	
25	Perform gemba walk	
26	Reward and recognition plan developed	

Chapter 13

Implementation Tools and Approaches

Typical Implementation Timeline

This timeline is presented to the work that occurs during the 12 weeks and to be able to use to judge progress during an implementation. If an organization is not using the Shengo method, some elements such as full work analysis (FWA) would be removed from the timeline. I would also caution the reader not to attempt a Lean implementation using this template without internal Lean experts or consultative services available (Table 13.1).

Gemba Walks

What follows is a simple guide for those who will be doing gemba walks (Table 13.2).

Cross-Training Matrix

A cross-training matrix is used to assess individuals' job skills and the training needed to improve their skills for a particular work process. In the example provided, medical records were used. So, the department leader would define all the duties carried out in medical records, then jointly assess with the individual employees regarding their skill levels for that particular job. Once completed, it can be the basis for a training program to cross-train staff in certain jobs (in the case of medical records, perhaps all jobs). Improving all staff work skills is an important component of balancing the load so, when staffs have idle time, they can help others. The rationale is also to cross train staff so that the work needs created by staff shortages can be addressed by others rather than having to hire PRN staff for temporary work (Figure 13.1). The categories include

Table 13.1 Implementation Timeline

Week	-4	-3	-2	-1	1	2	3	4	5	6	7	8	9	10	11	12
Project charter created and approved	■	■	■	■												
Lean culture survey	■	■	■	■												
Core team go to gemba	■	■	■	■												
Obtain history of clinic (physician, management, staff, culture, etc.)	■	■	■	■												
Core team takes photos	■	■	■	■												
Identify locations for info/metric boards	■	■	■	■												
Establish communication plans	■	■	■	■												
Establish training plans	■	■	■	■												
Project team—team leader, core team members, and site team members identified	■	■	■	■												
Project plan timeline developed and presented	■	■	■	■												
Baseline measures identified	■	■	■	■												
Team ground rules, expectations, roles, and responsibilities shared and accepted					■											
Implement communication plan					■											
Gemba—site team to go see and understand the baseline situation					■											
Create value stream map (VSM)					■	■										

Task	1	2	3	4	5	6	7	8	9	10	11	12
Baseline performance analysis	■											
Stakeholder analysis	■											
Provider meeting—standard work in exam and procedure rooms (equipment, supplies, forms)	■											
Install info/metric boards	■											
Site team orientation training including 6S	■											
2 h/4 h staff training sessions	■											
Cross-training matrix (give skeleton and develop with staff)	■											
Initiate product process flows (PPF)	■											
Implement communication plan	■											
Full work (operator) analysis	■	■										
Product process flow	■	■	■									
Weekly Lean site team meetings	■	■	■	■	■	■	■	■	■	■	■	■
Pilot or test potential new layouts			■									
Analyze demand requirements			■									
Create an assessment plan												
Cross-training matrix (drafted by site previous week and in place in at least one of area of department)				■								
6S training for all staff				■								

(Continued)

Table 13.1 Implementation Timeline (Continued)

Week	−4	−3	−2	−1	1	2	3	4	5	6	7	8	9	10	11	12
Tollgate								■								
Deadline: provider input on standard exam rooms								■								
Value stream map future state									■							
Ten-cycle analysis									■							
Introduction to pilot Kanban process									■							
6S implementation with assessment									■	■	■	■	■	■	■	■
Gather site team to pilot 6S mock up of common area									■							
Develop labor and capacity requirements									■							
Labor analysis training									■							
PDSA training									■							
Kanban training and implementation									■	■	■	■	■	■	■	■
Create standard work										■						
Identify recommendations from pilot programs										■						
Huddle boards used in all departments										■	■	■	■	■	■	■
Labor analysis conducted										■						
Implement Kanban										■	■	■	■	■	■	■
Implement standard exam rooms										■	■	■	■	■	■	■

Implement mistake-proof ideas	■	■	■	■	■	■
Implement visual controls	■	■	■	■	■	■
Training: managing in a Lean environment	■	■	■	■	■	■
Standard work assessments	■	■	■	■	■	■
Suggestions management system in place	■	■	■	■	■	■
Tollgate					■	
Site independently initiates and conducts daily huddles	■	■	■	■		
Project prioritization process in placed and managed by site Lean team and management	■	■	■	■		
Site management independently leads weekly Lean site meetings	■	■	■			
Sustain plan developed	■	■				
Baseline performance analysis with % changed to baseline						

Table 13.2   Gemba Walks

Why go to the gemba? Going to the gemba allows you to honestly evaluate work processes. Observing the work process helps you to "see"—with new eyes—all the challenges and problems the frontline staff encounters daily. Successful managers understand the processes before engaging frontline staff in problem resolution.
Who should go to the gemba? • Site team • Site leaders • Supervisors • Managers • Physicians
Where do I start? Begin at the first step of an identified process flow, and then walk through the entire process from start to finish. This is a simple way to notice key issues with single piece flow or batching, as well as identify priorities (or lack thereof).
What should I observe? It's important to have a clear and obvious focus. If you look for everything you'll likely accomplish nothing, as well as confuse priorities. Ask questions (don't tell). By asking questions, you encourage employees to understand the importance of their work. Select a different theme for every gemba walk. You will uncover all the important aspects of running your area. For example: • Understanding safety • Cost savings • People development • Quality • Reducing cycle times • Decreasing variation • Eliminating waste
When do I observe? Observing on a regular daily basis will send clear intentions that consistently demonstrate your commitment, and support of the continuous improvement process.
What do I do with my observations and learnings? Problems identified should be placed in the project prioritization matrix associated with the improvement board. Other employee and behavioral issues should be handled through traditional management mechanisms.

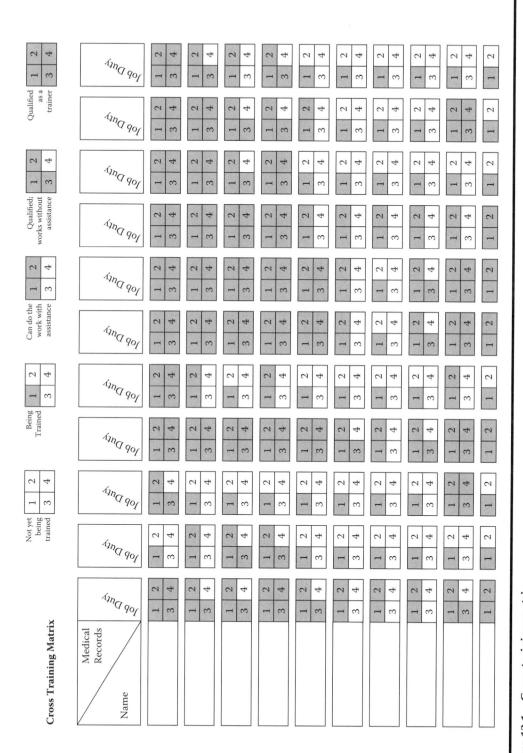

Figure 13.1   Cross training matrix.

- No training
- Being trained
- Can do the work with some assistance
- Qualified: can work independently
- Can function as a trainer

This tool should be used and updated periodically on an indefinite basis.

Glossary

Assessments (audits): Performed at least daily, assessments include a structured form containing items to be reviewed regarding a particular process. In addition to visual controls, it is a methodology to ensure that a process is functioning as expected.

Batching: Doing work or moving material in quantities greater than one, such as completing documentation in charts at the end of the day. Batching usually connotes waste, and should be eliminated. There are times when minimal batching is necessary.

Brownfield: The name given to existing operations, particularly when they are in the process of being converted from batch-and-queue production to lean productions. Brownfield operations already have established practices and cultures that are generally not effective. A Brownfield can only improve. Greenfields have no history, no culture, and no preexisting practices.

Defects: A type of waste where something was not done right the first time. Can apply to products in a process (lost lab result or medication error) or to the process itself (a treatment order is not sent by a physician's office, delaying treatment). Defects lead to rework, and more importantly, patient harm or death.

FIFO: First-in, first-out. Describing the type of flow of materials or people in a system in which the item that has been in inventory the longest is used first, or the patient who has been waiting the longest is seen first. The first patient request should be responded to first.

Six S (6S): Sort, shine, set in order, standardize, sustain, safety. These are five steps to remove unneeded tools, materials, debris, and clutter; thoroughly clean the entire areas and everything in it; establish a logical place for each item; mark locations for each place and the things that go in it; and establish a system to maintain the cleanliness and order you have established. With 5S, everything has a place, and you can tell at a glance what is supposed to be where, what does not belong in an area, what belongs, but is missing or out of place. It is one form of basic discipline. The concept of safety has been added by some, and refers to identifying potential safety hazards and correcting them.

Flow: The absence of waiting in a value stream. See also one piece flow.

Future state: Version of a value stream map that shows how things can, should, or will work in the future.

Gemba: Japanese word that means "the actual place" or "the place where the work is done."

Heijunka: Japanese word that means "level loading," either demand for a service or the workload for people in a system. A completely level-loaded system would have the same patient volumes or workloads in every time increment.

Ideal state: Version of a future state value stream map that shows how things should work, given ideal circumstances and processes.

Kaizen: Japanese word meaning "continuous improvement" or "small changes for the good."

Kaizen **event:** A formally defined event, typically 1–5 days long, with a team being formed to analyze the current process and make improvements in a process or value stream, with the team being disbanded after the event.

Kanban: A Japanese word that is translated as "signal" or "card," a method for managing and controlling the movement and ordering of materials in a system. Kanban cards contain the specific instructions regarding when to order and how much to order of a particular item. The cards are located with the item at the point of use.

Lean: A quality and process improvement methodology, based on the Toyota Production System, that emphasizes customer needs, improving quality, and reducing time delays and costs, all through continuous improvement and employee involvement.

Lean management system: The practices and tools used to monitor, measure, and sustain the operation of Lean production operations. Lean management practices identify where actual performance fails to meet expected performance; assigns and follows up improvement activities to bring actual performance in line with expected performance, or to raise the level of expected performance. The basic components of the Lean management system are standard work for leaders, visual controls, and a daily accountability process.

Non-value-added: A term that describes an activity that fails one or more of the three conditions for being value-added: (1) the patient is willing to pay for it (if he or she can), (2) the patient is physically or emotionally changed, and (3) it is done right the first time.

One piece flow (single piece flow): A Lean ideal where patients or products are treated, worked on, or moved one at a time. Single piece flow is an ultimate direction or goal that often cannot be attained without multiple process improvement attempts to reduce batch size.

Overprocessing: Doing more work than is necessary for good patient care or for customer needs. For example, spinning tubes of blood longer than necessary in a centrifuge does not lead to better test results; the unnecessary time is overprocessing. Asking patients repeatedly for the same information in a single encounter is another example.

Overproduction: Doing work earlier than is needed by the customer or creating items or materials that are not needed. An example is more flu shots than are needed for an immunization clinic.

PDSA (PDCA): Plan-Do-Study-Act (or Plan-Do-Check-Act). A continuous improvement cycle, similar to the scientific method and clinical decision making.

Pull: Used in Lean production systems where flow is not practical; pull production is based on replenishing what has been used by a customer. Grocery stores were among the first to adopt the process. When a grocery item is scanned through a bar code reader at checkout, the information is collected electronically. When the levels of stock reach a predetermined level, more of the item is ordered. A pull system in healthcare would be one where patients could have exactly what they want, when they want it.

Standard work for leaders: One of the key elements of the Lean management system, standard work for leaders specifies the actions to be taken each day to focus on the processes in each leader's area of responsibility.

Standardized work: Specifications, usually for a process or the job tasks for a particular type of employee, that include the sequence in which steps or work elements are performed, expected time needed for each element, and the total time needed for the entire process. Standard work in a laboratory might include all the steps for running a test and the time required to complete each step. Standard work for a nurse might include preparation for the work day (shift), quality checks, patient preparation, etc.

Toyota Production System (TPS): Developed over the past 50 years at Toyota, based initially on the writings of Henry Ford. TPS seeks to eliminate waste from production processes. The ideal approach in TPS is for production to operate at exactly the rate of customer demand. This is often expressed in Just-in-Time production, where nothing is produced until there is specific customer demand for it. See also Pull, and Flow.

Value stream: The people and equipment involved in producing a healthcare service or product. Value streams usually include each of the subprocesses and equipment needed to produce a service for a patient. The intent is to minimize the distance people have to move and maximize the speed of flow through the production process.

Visual controls: Visual controls are the variety of approaches that make the status of a process visible at a glance. They include production-tracking charts of various kinds that show actual versus expected performance. Hour by day charts for a PACU and patients seen per hour are examples. Strictly speaking, visual controls allow for control of processes rather than actually exerting control themselves.

Waste: Activity that does not add value for the customer or patient. Synonymous with non-value-added.

Index

About the Author

Mike Nelson spent 28 years practicing pediatrics while building the practice from a solo physician office to seven pediatricians. He has served as a hospital medical staff president and in various medical director positions. For the last 13 years, he has devoted increasingly greater time to quality improvement in healthcare. For the last 5 years of employment with Presbyterian Healthcare Services, he worked full time in quality improvement and became a certified Lean Six Sigma Black Belt. He was a physician leader for Lean Systems implementation at Presbyterian.

He is credited with:

- Creating a health and chronic disease management system resulting in national benchmark performance in diabetes care
- Developing a curriculum and teaching more than 200 clinicians and senior leaders advanced tools and techniques in quality improvement
- Implementing elements of the advanced medical home
- Creating a patient-centered care environment through the creation of patient and family advisory councils in PMG clinics
- Leading and supporting successful Lean implementations resulting in dramatic improvements in ambulatory clinics and inpatient settings

He currently owns a Lean consulting business, Blue Corn Professional Services, LLC, and is a physician coach for the Studer Group.